# GUERRILLA MARKETING

# JOB ESCAPE PLAN

The Ten Battles You Must Fight to Start Your Own Business,
and HOW TO WIN Them Decisively

# JAY CONRAD LEVINSON
# & ANDREW NEITLICH

NEW YORK

# GUERRILLA MARKETING
## Job Escape Plan

**The Ten Battles You Must Fight to Start Your Own Business,
and HOW TO WIN Them Decisively**

## JAY CONRAD LEVINSON
## & ANDREW NEITLICH

© 2011 Jay Conrad Levinson and Andrew Neitlich. All rights reserved.

ISBN 978-1-61448-014-3 Paperback
ISBN 978-1-61448-015-0 eBook
Library of Congress Control Number

Published by:
**MORGAN JAMES PUBLISHING**
The Entrepreneurial Publisher
5 Penn Plaza, 23rd Floor
New York City, New York 10001
(212) 655-5470 Office
(516) 908-4496 Fax
www.MorganJamesPublishing.com

**Cover Design by:**
Rachel Lopez
rachel@r2cdesign.com

**Interior Design by:**
Bonnie Bushman
bbushman@bresnan.net

In an effort to support local communities, raise awareness and funds, Morgan James Publishing donates one percent of all book sales for the life of each book to Habitat for Humanity.
Get involved today, visit
**www.HelpHabitatForHumanity.org.**

*For everyone*
*with the courage*
*and passion*
*to live life*
*on their terms.*

**Also by Jay Conrad Levinson
and Andrew Neitlich:**

# GUERRILLA MARKETING FOR A BULLETPROOF CAREER:
How to Attract Ongoing Opportunities in
Perpetually Gut-Wrenching Times,
for Entrepreneurs, Employees,
and Everyone in Between

# CONTENTS

# ACKNOWLEDGEMENTS

## JAY CONRAD LEVINSON

I owe heartfelt acknowledgement in this book to Andrew Neitlich, who did all the heavy lifting and supplied the brilliance with which this book has been written. If you benefit from his insight, give all the credit to him, for I was merely along for the ride. My main contribution has been to provide the guerrilla spirit that has infused him. He has done a wonderful job of absorbing it and spreading it to everyone who reads the words he has written.

## ANDREW NEITLICH

I remain forever grateful to Jim Reilly, who was generous enough to introduce me to Jay Conrad Levinson. Jay has been a hero of mine for decades, and it continues to be an honor and a highlight of my career to have this opportunity to work with him on a second book. Special thanks are due to www.HelpAReporter.com for putting me in touch with a terrific network of people who quit their jobs to start businesses. Thank you also to the many entrepreneurs who were willing to share their experiences in this book. Eternal thanks go to my wife Elena, for all that she does to keep our family going while I write and grow my businesses; I will never fully understand how she can do all that she does to get the kids ready for everything they are doing, keep the house running smoothly, cook gourmet meals, continue to get better at tennis, and run her own successful business. No married entrepreneur can succeed in business without a supportive spouse, and I am blessed that I am married to Elena. Finally, I want to acknowledge my children Noah, Seth, and Willow, and wish them satisfaction, joy, peace, and success.

# PREFACE
## by Jay Conrad Levinson

It is a pure joy to work with Andrew. The reason is because he dreamt the dream and now lives the dream. He talks the talk, as you'll learn as you read these pages, and he walks the walk, as you'll discover as you experience the joy of self-employment through his eyes.

Because I have trod the same path, I have more than an inkling of what Andrew is talking about and I can attest that he is speaking the truth with every sentence and every word he writes. As one who followed Andrew's sage advice before he even offered it, I learned that mastering the possible is not easy, but it is always worth the effort.

To help people reap lush rewards for their effort, I wrote the first Guerrilla Marketing book, and now we have put the notion of Guerrilla Marketing into more than 21 million minds, for that is how many books we have sold on the topic.

Guerrilla Marketing has shown entrepreneurs how to succeed with creative, resourceful, low-cost marketing tactics. It has made Guerrilla Marketing a household word around the planet. However, until now, no Guerrilla Marketing book has shown how to go from being an employee to becoming a business owner. Thanks to Andrew, here is a book that can do that.

Thanks once more to Andrew, today, no one has to tolerate a lousy job or boss anymore. Anyone can break free in a matter of weeks, or even months. Is it easy? It is not. Is it possible? You can be sure that it is. Both Andrew and I are assured of that every minute of every day.

There is a revolution in going solo and starting businesses, thanks to the Internet and to the social media. There is a corresponding decline in loyalty and benefits from employers, as there are now more benefits than ever in working on our own. Truth is, it has never been so simple and so available. Never before have there been so many real-life role models.

This book shows you how to gain the indescribably joyous independence of going it on your own, while focusing on ten battles required to escape your job once and for all. Make no mistake: There are battles, and you must win each one. I've been doing it, working from my home since 1971, learning as I go along, and having the privilege of being able to relate my experiences to your life. Pay close attention: This is non-fiction.

It surely wasn't easy all along and there certainly were setbacks. But the setbacks seem diminished with time and the triumphs were sweeter than ever. The biggest lesson I learned along the way is that people don't fail—they simply stop trying. I never stopped trying and my enjoyment of life was ample payback for the hard work I did invest. The mere knowledge that my weekends begin late Wednesday afternoon was the carrot at the end of my stick that motivated me to move forward.

In nature, nothing ever retires, so I was never tempted to fall into the retirement trap. As one who has toiled like crazy on Mondays, Tuesdays, and Wednesdays only, I have considered myself retired since I lived by the enlightenment Andrew relates here—back in June of 1971. What a ride!

I learned, as you will learn too, that being a successful entrepreneur and a winning guerrilla marketer is not a spectator sport. To do those things requires action. The world now belongs to those who can dream and then give wings to their dreams with action. Without the action the dreams remain castles in the air, without foundations. Please absorb this and let it stick to the ribs of your mind: You can't just dream; you must take action.

While you are making the leap from employment to freedom, you will meet all sorts of people who are there to support you, cheer you on, and help you. This book is filled with examples of such people and with people such as you can be. Andrew and I are two such people.

Both of us wish you the best of success. We are confident that you will attain, and then surpass, your goal.

**Jay Conrad Levinson**
*DeBary, Florida*

# INTRODUCTION:
## Yes, You Can Do This!

es, you can do this. You can quit your job, start a business, and never have to work for anybody else ever again. You can do this regardless of....

- Whether you feel confident or afraid.
- Whether you are young or old.
- Whether you have a family to support or are single.
- Whether you have an advanced degree or don't even have your GED.
- Whether you live in a congested city or in the middle of nowhere.
- Whether you have an MBA or don't know a thing about starting a business.
- Whether you don't have much time or have lots of it.
- Whether you have lots of money to invest or little cash to spare.

There is always a way, if you want it badly enough. You don't have to tolerate a crummy job, lousy boss, long commute, tedious tasks, annoying co-workers, limited control over how you spend your day, no clear path to a promotion, worrying about the next round of layoffs, dealing with corporate scandals that have nothing to do with you, reporting to an executive team that you don't like or trust...You can leave all this behind!

Once you do, you probably will never want to go back. You won't believe you waited so long. You will open up a whole new world filled with wonderful opportunities, dynamic people, and creative freedom. You will feel more in control of when you work, where you work, how you work, with whom you work, and where you take your company…in other words, your destiny.

I know that you can do this, because I have done it and because millions of other people have done it, too. We are ordinary people, although the way that we got here differs. Based on my interviews with hundreds of entrepreneurs, we have escaped our jobs for different reasons and in different ways, including:

- **Agonize for what seems like forever, and then get started.** I am the poster child for this story. Since taking my first job out of college, I constantly dreamt up new business ideas, to the point that one of my performance reviews docked me for talking openly about my desire to start a business. I didn't like working for other people. I couldn't stand the routine of working in an 8 am to 6 pm job. But I was afraid to break out on my own. I didn't do much more than talk about my ideas, or write up academic business plans that I could never get funded. I was waiting for someday, as if I didn't have to actually do anything to wake up one morning and discover that, magically, I owned my own very profitable business. As time passed and my family responsibilities increased, I got even more afraid. Eventually, I reported to a CEO who I thought was a fool. I knew that if he could start a successful company with his skill set, then I definitely could with mine. That sense of confidence, plus the bursting of the dot-com bubble, caused me to start moonlighting to start up my own consulting business. Within six months I was laid off, but with enough clients to replace half of my previous salary. A year later, I was earning more than what I did in my last job.

- **Start a business almost by accident.** Brianna Sylver didn't mean to start a business. She kept looking for the right job in strategic product design and development, but the offers she got weren't a perfect fit. Nevertheless, her prospective employers often hired her as a consultant, even though they agreed with her that a full-time job wasn't right. Finally, she did get that perfect job offer and turned it down anyway. "At that point, I decided that I had a company." Now she has a blossoming company with a team of 14.

- **Start a business because your back is against the wall.** The legendary general Sun Tzu would often place his soldiers in horribly dangerous positions, for instance, with their backs to a vertical cliff so that they could only escape by going through the enemy. That way, their life depended on defeating the enemy and they would fight accordingly. Many entrepreneurs start a job either right after they are laid off, or when they see a layoff coming. Some even quit their jobs so that they have no choice but to succeed. If your back is against the wall, it is amazing what you can do. For instance, Sean Bryant, founder of FreeSnatcher.com, started his company because he realized that his position at a major bank was on the brink of being eliminated. At the same time, due to the difficult economy, he recognized an immediate need for an outlet that would provide families with tips and sources necessary to successfully save money. Now that Sean has a taste of being his own boss, he says he'll never go back to corporate America again. He plans to continue growing FreeSnatcher.com to be bigger and better than ever with a plethora of money-saving tips and deals.

- **Grow a company after grabbing a single opportunity.** Patricia Kilgore led the marketing and communications department for a major company. A new CEO told her to outsource the department. After lots of soul searching, she proposed to the CEO that she start up her own firm to handle the company's marketing needs. Her former employer became her first client. Years later, although she is no longer working with that original client, she runs a $2 million marketing and public relations firm.

- **Stop being sick and tired of corporate culture and politics.** I can't count how many entrepreneurs told me that they started their businesses because they were tired of all of the junk that they had to put up with when they worked for a large employer. One wonders if the top executives at big companies will ever be able to create a culture that eliminates the hassles of getting things done while dealing with inertia, bureaucracy, and dysfunctional behaviors.

- **Let a side venture grow, and then take the leap when it is successful enough.** Chris Brusznicki, co-founder of GameDayHousing.com left a lucrative job at Goldman Sachs to run his business full-time. He started the venture as a MBA student at Northwestern, when he rented out an investment property near Notre Dame stadium to alumni returning for football games. After building up a portfolio of six properties with a business partner, he created an online website to broker game-day rentals for other property owners. The company brokered well over $1 million in rentals in its first year of operations and is doubling in business every month. While some might think Chris is crazy to have left a job at one of the few companies that offers a nearly guaranteed way for employees to get rich, he's not looking back.

- **Take advantage of youth and lack of responsibilities.** Anybody of any age can start a successful business; however, many younger entrepreneurs take advantage of their youth and relative freedom. What better time to start a business than when you don't have a family to care for and your expenses are relatively low?

- **Make more money on your own, because you know you can.** Susan Dawson worked as an associate for a law firm and realized two things. First, she was bringing in much more in billings than the firm was paying her in salary. Second, the law firm wasn't going to elevate her to partner based on her ability to bring in work. She did the logical thing and started her own firm, WP&D. Now she makes a lot more money, while enjoying much more flexibility to care for her children than she ever did working for someone else's firm.

- **Start a company because you can do it better than your employer.** Rusty Sena, owner of the prepress company Echelon, is a classic example: "I worked for one of the larger companies in Los Angeles. I eventually got fed up with how things were run and thought I could do it better, and so did my business partner. We bitched about it so much we thought it would be better to stop bitching and do something. Hence our company was born."

Similarly, Steven Street of Abeyta Street Accurate Process Services, Inc. writes, "I was the manager of a large process serving company. During my last year as the manager of that company, I closely watched and studied my boss and the way he ran his business, including the policies that he enacted to regulate his business and his employees. There were many rules and policies that I fundamentally disagreed with, and I felt I could do a much better job handling the business and my employees to build a company. After speaking with family, colleagues, and friends, the same message was presented to me again and again: I needed to step outside of my comfort zone, and there was no better time than the present. So I went for it and landed a large law firm as my client, and I am much happier today than I ever was working for someone else."

- **Get tired of saying, "Yes, and may I please have another?"** Lots of people get sick and tired of dealing with abuse and lousy bosses, and so they do their own thing. For instance, Bobby MacDonald of VegasBottle. com shares, "Upon being recruited as an entry-level employee for one of the major public accounting firms, I was sold on their prestigious reputation and the respect that I instantly acquired when telling friends and family about my new career. However, once I began the job and came to understand the level of disrespect I would receive as a new employee and the sheer amount of ass-kissing I was expected to dole out to superiors, that rosy outlook turned to certain dismay. I fully dreaded going to work each day and began to work doubly hard on my budding Internet marketing side business, even while purporting to do accounting busywork in the office. After one full year of hell, my side business was finally paying more than my regular salary... so I packed up my stuff, said goodbye to the crash dummies working at my office, and moved to a more tropical location. Though working for yourself can be challenging, I have not regretted the move for even an instant."

- **Adapt to a life change.** Having a baby, having kids leave for college, going through a divorce, and dealing with a difficult disease can all lead to starting a new business. Lisa Zollinger was tired of working the long hours that the world of newspapers demanded, especially when her child turned five years old. She also had a passion for teaching art, and started researching ways to do that. When she found Young Rembrandts, a franchise that offers after-school art education programs to kids, she jumped at the opportunity and bought a territory. "I knew immediately that this was what I wanted to do," she says.

Christine Clifford started her business after being diagnosed with cancer: "I was the top salesperson in the multi-million dollar retail services industry for a New York based company. It was an enormously stressful job, and one that required constant traveling, having spent 298 nights on the road that year. Diagnosed with breast cancer, my life came to a screeching halt. I stepped back and decided, 'I don't want to do this anymore. My health has got to be my #1 priority.' I left to start The Cancer Club, www.cancerclub.com, today the world's largest producer of humorous and helpful products for people with cancer. I went on to write six award-winning books about my story, including my best seller *Not Now...I'm Having a No Hair Day!* I've been self employed now for fifteen years, and have never looked back."

- **Do it because your life would be painfully incomplete if you didn't.** Some people start companies because they were born to be entrepreneurs, and that's that. Either they've always wanted to start a company and finally take the leap, or they have a sudden realization that they want to start a business. Sue Markgraf enjoyed her position as manager of public relations with the Chicago Botanic Garden. She woke up one morning, looked out the window and thought to herself, "I love my job. I could probably retire from here." The thought sent her into a mild panic attack. From an entrepreneurial family, she realized that her passion really was in starting her own firm. Her life would be incomplete if she didn't. Now she runs GreenMark Public Relations, which specializes in serving clients representing green spaces, places and issues.

- **Do something bold.** Would you be crazy enough to start a new pizza chain in a city famous for great pizza restaurants? Eric Fosse did when he started the Homemade Pizza Company in Chicago. He shares, "The idea was pig-headed. I wanted to prove that I could succeed here. Chicago is known for pizza. If we could establish ourselves here, it would mean something." He worked on different dough recipes in his brother's basement for two years before launching his first take-home pizza store. As I write this, he is opening his 30th store and operates in two other markets outside of Chicago.

- **Find a niche to serve.** Andrew Dennis had a lucrative job with The Chicago Board of Trade, but he always wanted to start his own business. He became interested in websites like priceline.com and hotels.com that focused on unsold inventory, and started to research other niches where this concept could work. Restaurant reservations had been done. Golf course reservations had been done. Eventually he found an untapped niche in the spa and salon market, and created the site www.spaciety.com to offer discounts to consumers looking for spa and salon treatments.

You might fit into one of the above categories, or into an entirely new category of your own. Whatever your story, you can do it, if you want to. This book shows you how. It isolates the key attitudes, thought process, decisions, and actions you need in place to make the leap. Unlike other books about starting a business, this book focuses exclusively on the immediate things you need to think about and do RIGHT NOW—while you are between deciding to take the leap and actually taking it.

Following the *Guerrilla Marketing* metaphor, it describes ten battles you have to fight—and win—to successfully escape your job and go out on your own. Some readers might find only a few of these battles to be challenging. Others might find all of them to be worthy fights, as I did when I took the leap.

The ten battles include:

- **Battle Number One: Win The Mental Battle.** Embrace the mindsets of the entrepreneur.

- **Battle Number Two: Come Up with a Workable Idea.** There are almost unlimited sources for business ideas, and many are right in front of your face.

- **Battle Number Three: Get Strong Support from Friends, Family, and Your Network.** You can't succeed without support.

- **Battle Number Four: Develop a Strategy That Gives You an Edge.** Every business needs an edge in order to stand out and attract fickle, skeptical customers.

- **Battle Number Five: Define a Pathway to Profits.** If you don't have a way to make a profit and pay your salary, you have a hobby, not a business.

- **Battle Number Six: Generate Enough Cash to Give Yourself a Chance.** You can always be resourceful while bootstrapping your business. At the same time, set yourself up with enough reserves so that you don't feel panicked and so that you can give your business the fair chance it deserves.

- **Battle Number Seven: Master Your Time.** Lots of people say they want to start a business, but if you study how they spend their time, you can see that they are not serious. What about you?

- **Battle Number Eight: Get Top Talent on Your Team.** You don't necessarily need employees when you first start out, but you do need a team of talented people to help you.

- **Battle Number Nine: Achieve Quick, Low-Risk Successes To Get Your First Profitable Customer.** Don't risk it all right out of the gate! Start slowly and learn. Your business will grow organically and be stronger as a result.

- **Battle Number Ten: Keep Going Until The Business Achieves Momentum.** The first customer is only a start. Now you have build on that success and achieve true momentum.

The book concludes with a step-by-step plan for you to make the leap gracefully, on your terms, along with advice from other entrepreneurs who are cheering for you.

Note that my goal in writing this book with Jay is to have at least ONE MILLION people start successful businesses and quit their jobs forever. I'm not kidding. I want to see ONE MILLION people take action to create the life they want and deserve. To achieve that goal, I have created the Job Escape Challenge. Here's how it works: You have the book. Now I challenge you to take action and live your dreams—and I'm willing to help in any way I can. Towards that end, I am going to give you many more tools than a book alone can provide. Log into www.JobEscapePlan.com at any time, and use the pass code ESCAPE. This exclusive member area gives you additional great tools for you to plan your escape, get your questions answered, and keep moving forward even when you don't feel like it. I sincerely hope you accept my challenge and will use these tools to start your business and escape your job.

Once again: You can do this. It might end up being hard or easy. It might take a long time or happen more quickly than you had expected. What matters is that you can do this. I wish you the best of success while you live your dreams and bring your business to life.

# SPECIAL REPORT
## Before You Start: Know Your Legal Obligations to Your Employer

Before you start your business, make sure you aren't doing anything that might have legal repercussions with your current employer. The last thing you want to do is get sued by a company that has more resources to spend on lawyers than you do, especially after you pour your heart and soul into a new venture that has potential. If in doubt, get some legal advice of your own, and be up front with your company about your intentions.

- If you accepted a signing bonus, or if your company paid for your schooling, sometimes you have to agree to stay a certain period of time or be liable to pay your company back.

- Check the terms of any non-compete and confidentiality agreements, and make sure nothing you do in your new business violates those terms.

- Some companies ask employees to sign a statement that they will not engage in any commercial activity outside of their employment. If you signed such a clause, you need to negotiate a waiver with your employer.

- Watch out for any potential conflicts of interest. For instance, be especially careful about poaching—or even appearing to poach—customers, employees, and even vendors from your company, especially while you still work there.

- Don't use any company time or resources to start up your business. Otherwise, the company can claim that they own any intellectual property that you create.

- Be extremely cautious about anything you do on your work computer and mobile devices. Don't send emails or texts about your new business, conduct business on company devices, or store any files about your business on your work computer. At the same time, don't transfer any company information to your personal email box, because that can be construed as stealing company secrets.

- Use discretion while getting your business up and running. Even if you have a good personal relationship with your colleagues and boss, keep the business in stealth mode and avoid discussing it at work. Be cautious about what you post on your social media pages. This is as much a legal issue as a political and etiquette issue. People who like their job, or who don't like their job but can't seem to do anything about it, will resent you when you gush about how exciting your new business venture is. Your boss might feel like you are not putting all of your effort into your job and even fire you. Leave on your terms, not somebody else's whim.

## Chapter One

# BATTLE NUMBER ONE:
## Win the Mental Battle

Entrepreneurs think differently than people who are content to be employees. Their mindsets give them the courage and fortitude to create a business from scratch, to overcome significant obstacles, and to handle issues that most employees never have to consider. Before you escape your job, you need to embrace the attitudes of the entrepreneur. Once you do, you have won your first and perhaps most challenging battle on your way to self-employment.

Following are twelve attitudes for you to win the mental battle.

---

### THE TWELVE MINDSETS REQUIRED TO WIN BATTLE NUMBER ONE,
#### The Mental Battle

One: Get rid of any misperceptions about owning a business.

Two: I can do this.

Three: Be open to advice and help.

Four: See lucrative opportunities when others don't.

Five: Tolerate imperfection.

Six: Improvise with finesse, especially in the face of limited resources.

Seven: Minimize risk and downside while maximizing upside.

Eight: Influence others.

Nine: Develop thick skin.

Ten: Keep moving forward, regardless of how you feel at the moment.

Eleven: Think critically about the business, without drinking the Kool-Aid.

Twelve: Take 100 percent responsibility.

---

# MINDSET ONE: GET RID OF ANY MISPERCEPTIONS ABOUT OWNING A BUSINESS.

There are many myths about running your own business. If you believe them, you will quickly become frustrated and perhaps even quit. Here are a few:

- **Business is a glamorous, romantic adventure.** When you first start your business, nobody is going to ooh and ahhh simply because you have a business card with a prestigious title like CEO or Principal. Investing in fancy furniture and office space, getting health insurance, and taking a long vacation may not be possible for a while. Local and national media probably won't be lining up any time soon to interview you for a front-page feature. Instead, expect to roll up your sleeves and get your hands dirty while you make a name for yourself and your business. Until your business gets momentum and you can afford to hire people, you are chief salesman, product shipper, IT guy, shipping clerk, administrative assistant, intern, bookkeeper, government liaison, and janitor all in one. You handle mundane issues that most employees never have to worry about. For instance, my wife Elena is a stay-at-home mom with a successful etiquette training business, and she often takes phone calls in the car outside our house, with our baby nursing on her lap, while I watch the older kids inside the house. There's not a lot of glamour in that!

- **You have more time.** Timothy Ferriss' *The Four-Hour Work Week* offers a wonderful aspiration after you get your feet on the ground as a business owner. However, most entrepreneurs I interviewed repeated the same theme: When you quit your job and start a business, you trade a 40-hour workweek for an 80-hour workweek. Don't start a business if you aren't ready to dedicate your full time and attention to it.

- **You make more money than you do as an employee.** As the infomercial disclaimers say, "You could earn less or much, much more." Eventually you can make more money, but initially you may not. When you quit a job, you lose a regular source of income and any health insurance and other benefits that come with it. Many entrepreneurs never make what they did while employed, and they don't care because they love working on their own. Others need to grow their business over a year or two before they match their former salary. Some exceed their salary within a few months of quitting their jobs, usually because they built up the business in their spare time. There are no guarantees.

- **You have more freedom.** As an entrepreneur, you have the freedom to choose your customers, how you spend your time, where you work, with whom you work, how you dress, and which initiatives get priority. However, freedom requires discipline, and some people can't handle all of the choices that freedom brings. You need to structure your day so that you do what needs to be done. Also, as entrepreneur Brianna Sylver shares, "You have freedom and flexibility as an entrepreneur but not predictability. For instance, you might decide to go on vacation, but if something comes up with your business, you either don't take the vacation or work during your vacation."

- **It's all sunshine and daisies.** Some people are so miserable in their current jobs that they imagine only the upside of owning their own business. The truth is that most entrepreneurs face both extreme highs and lows before they get their business off the ground. Lows include struggling to pay your bills, getting rejected again and again, testing products and services that don't succeed, wondering whether you ever should have taken the leap, and worrying about what your family will think if you fail. The highs are great, but don't go into business if you can't handle the lows.

- **You are not accountable to anyone else and you can do whatever you want.** If anything, you are more accountable when you run your own business than when you are an employee. You are accountable to the IRS for taxes, to all levels of government and their regulations, to your customers for the promises you make, to any investors and lenders, to any employees and contractors who count on you for their paycheck, to your vendors for their fees, and to your own and your family's needs. My first boss used to tell me that everyone has a boss: "If you are the CEO, you still report to your board of directors. If you don't have a board of directors, you still report to your customers. And if you have a spouse and kids, you always report to them."

- **You have enough money to grow your business.** Most people I interviewed for this book were clear: You will never have as much money as you really want to build your business. For instance, Eric Fosse of the Homemade Pizza Company said, "Everyone will tell you that you won't have enough money. They are right. You always need more." In other words, prepare to be creative and resourceful. The *Guerrilla Marketing* series of books has made one thing clear: Most entrepreneurs don't have unlimited dollars to invest in their business, but they can use their unlimited creativity, innovation, and street smarts to succeed in business…and these assets can go much further than a big bank account.

- **It is a pleasure to serve customers.** In reality, some customers will drive you crazy. They will waste your time with questions and never buy. They will appear to want something for nothing. They will buy something from you and then complain about it, even if you gave them exactly what you promised. Some will sue you, or threaten to sue you, for what seem to you like frivolous reasons. If customers are even mildly dissatisfied, they might post complaints about you all over the Internet, rather than work with you to resolve the issue. Many will lie to you throughout the sales process and even after they buy, supporting the old salesperson's maxim, "Buyers are liars." For instance, during the sales process, many people aren't honest about whether they have enough money to afford your products, whether they are really serious about buying, and whether they are serious about buying from you. They will tell you they are going to buy next week, and then delay or disappear. They will tell you they need to think things over, when they really mean, "Buzz off!" After someone buys from you and gets value from your products and services, be ready for some of them to try to get a full refund, claiming general dissatisfaction with no specific or valid reasons, or even breaking the merchandise on purpose. Expect bounced checks, identity fraud, and outright theft to take away some of your inventory. Again, most customers are wonderful, and legitimate complaints are important feedback about how you can improve your business. However, the most difficult customers can quickly suck your enjoyment out of the business if you don't have the right temperament. Don't go into business for yourself if you aren't mentally prepared for the reality of customer service, or if you aren't ready to use your best negotiating skills to avoid being a doormat.

- **The best product or most competent professional wins.** In a perfectly fair world, this statement would be true. But the world isn't fair. For better or for worse, the best product doesn't always win. The smartest, most skilled professional doesn't always get the job. Instead, the best marketer usually does. Therefore, go into business only if you are willing to spend your time marketing your business to attract new customers and sell more products and services to existing customers. If you think you can sit back and wait for customers to call, then employment might be a better fit for you.

- **You need a brilliant idea to start a business.** The mainstream media, business book market, and business school case studies tend to be biased in favor of the handful of businesses that aim to change the world. This bias might cause you to worry that your business isn't unique or ingenious enough. You do need to offer a valuable service and be able to differentiate your business while becoming visible in the marketplace. However, you can do this without inventing the next Dyson vacuum cleaner, Segway, DVR, or IMAX theatre. Every day entrepreneurs start successful businesses based on passion, competence, and hustle. You can, too.

- **A brilliant business plan means that you will have a successful business.** The entrepreneurs interviewed for this book didn't obsess over creating a thesis-style, brilliant business plan that would wow venture capitalists and get them a million-dollar investment. Instead, they roughed out some numbers and crafted a living, breathing plan—usually no more than a few pages—to get the business started, attract customers, delight those customers, and get enough cash coming in to get the business going. Entrepreneurs live in the real world, not in the world of book reports. Very few people ever need a fancy business plan ready for angels and venture capitalists; most of us have to bootstrap our businesses on our own. By all means, do your homework before you start your business. However, once you have 60 to 80 percent of the information you need, it is time to take action and test your business idea in the real world.

- **You take huge risks when you start a business.** It can feel scary to start a business, but you don't have to take huge risks. You don't have to put your life's savings or your family's wellbeing in jeopardy. In fact, as later chapters of this book will show, the smartest entrepreneurs don't risk much at all. There are many ways to test your business idea and get started without spending lots of money or quitting your job. Contrary to popular belief, it is more risky to have a job, because as an employee you have just one customer: your employer. When you own the business, you can spread your risk out over many customers.

- **If the business fails, you are a failure**. Wrong, wrong, and more wrong! If the business doesn't work out, you still have done something wonderful. You have taken a risk, lived on the edge, and had the courage to do something that most people only dream about. You can learn from your mistakes and start another business. You can always go back to work as an employee; in fact, employers might find you more valuable because of your experience. Meanwhile, chances are that you make all sorts of new connections while you work to start your business, connections you can't even imagine right now, and that these people will help you find new opportunities if things don't work out. You are not your business. Your business is one single, tiny expression of your passion, vision, power, and dreams. Don't get dramatic and turn it into something more than it really is.

## MINDSET TWO: I CAN DO THIS!

The mindset "I can do this!" means that you create possibility, generate resolve, and remain inspired—even in the face of daunting fear, uncertainty, limited knowledge, setbacks, and potential failure. Entrepreneurs create something from nothing. They start with an idea and create a viable business based on that idea, but that is only the beginning. They have a sense of possibility, resolve, and inspiration that few employees can fathom, and that allows them to persevere no matter what comes their way.

It all starts with a mindset of "I can do this!"—a firm belief that they can make something good appear even though nothing exists now.

Here is a metaphor that might help make this mindset come alive for you. Have you ever gone scuba diving in cold, deep, dark waters—for instance, off the coast of Maine? As you descend down the anchor line of the boat, something eerie happens. About 30 feet down, if you look down, you see your anchor line disappear into the dark depths of the water. If you look up, you see the anchor line disappear above you, too. You are floating in nothingness, a strange nowhere zone. Inexperienced divers often can't handle this situation. Sometimes they can't even tell which way is up or down—even though their bubbles float up and clearly point to the surface. A few divers panic and freeze up or waste all of their air supply breathing too quickly. Many signal to the dive master that they want to quit the dive and get back to the boat. However, those who have the resolve to continue get to enjoy a fantastic experience. As they keep descending down the anchor line, foot by foot, eventually something amazing starts to come into view—for instance, the hull of a Colonial-era ship that wrecked hundreds of years ago, along with a couple of giant lobsters keeping guard.

Entrepreneurs are able to keep diving past the nowhere zone until they reach their destination. They know that if they keep going, one step at a time, something good will appear. They stay resolved and keep saying, "I can do this," even though their anchor line has disappeared into the depths. Whatever the obstacle, they persist until they find a way over it, around it, under it, or through it.

Read the following situations. If you want to strike out on your own and escape the world of employment forever, you have to be able to generate the resolve to handle these issues and keep pressing forward. You have to keep thinking, "I can do this."

- You ask 20 people to buy your services or product, and all of them say no.
- You are ready to open for business, and the city building inspector refuses to grant you a certificate of occupancy until you make some costly changes.
- You tell people about your business idea, and they don't seem to understand it or know anyone who would become customers.
- You are short the cash you need for next week's payroll and have a week to figure out how to pay your employees.
- You spend six months training a promising employee in the business, and then he quits.
- Your biggest customer goes broke, leaving you with tens of thousands of dollars in unpaid invoices and reducing your revenues by 25 percent.
- You get a notice from the state telling you that you underpaid sales tax; now you need to come up with funds to pay what you owe, along with interest and penalties.

- Your China-based supplier, who requires payment up front before commencing manufacturing, sends you a shipment of defective products—and refuses to correct the errors unless you pay more money.

- You invest in a radio marketing campaign, and the results don't nearly pay back your investment; now you are stumped about how to become visible in your market and attract more customers.

- A competitor starts up and seems to offer the same products and services you do, but at lower prices.

You get the idea, right? As an employee, there are always other people around to handle these issues and motivate you to keep pressing forward. As an entrepreneur, you are the one who has to generate possibility and resolve so that these issues are dealt with. You are the first and the last to stay inspired, and that inspiration needs to be so infectious that it motivates others. When others have big doubts, you help them see a way forward. When things look bleak, you find a path to success. No matter how daunting the situation, you don't give up. You keep finding ways to move forward.

Here is another question to ask: When do you quit? Some would-be entrepreneurs quit after they hit their first minor obstacle. For instance, I met a woman who said to me, "I've really wanted to start a business for a year now, but I don't even know how to register my name or get the right licenses." For a full year, she hasn't started a business because of what is a non-issue to any serious entrepreneur. How likely do you think she will be to succeed, even if she does figure out how to name her business and go to the local town hall to fill out a form, pay a few dollars, and get a business license? Never mind her. What about you? Do you quit before you should?

Real entrepreneurs keep going in order to create a viable business. They find ways to get over obstacles, get hard-to-find information to make smart decisions, and deal with uncertainty. Of course, they aren't crazy. They don't bring their families to financial ruin pursuing a dumb idea. They do their homework. They minimize their risk. They set limits on the total amount of time and money they will invest in the venture before doing something else. Within those constraints, they have a sense of possibility and keep going.

## SPECIAL RESEARCH REPORT:
### Advice from Entrepreneurs About Dealing With Fear When Starting a Business

Following is a summary of research conducted through interviews with a number of business owners about dealing with fear when starting a business. These entrepreneurs shared the many different kinds of fear they experienced when they started: fear of financial ruin, fear of failure, fear of handling success, fear of rejection, fear of not living up to the expectations of loved ones, fear of criticism by customers, fear of not knowing enough, fear of being laughed at by their network, fear of feeling isolated, fear of having to start all over, fear of losing themselves in the business, and general fear of jumping into the unknown and the uncertain. Then they offered suggestions about how to handle these fears. Their advice falls into six categories, which you will see come up again and again in this book:

- **First, go into business prepared.** Do your homework. Have a plan. Know your industry. Save up some cash reserves, and be ready to spend twice what you think you will need to spend. Marketing consultant Karen Saverino, President of Eightfold Strategy, shares, "Before starting my company I saved up for a year's worth of living expenses. You hear this advice a lot and it works. You have to know that your basic needs and a few small luxuries will be covered in order to focus on your business success. Second, I had a solid business plan in place that included events, email marketing, direct outreach, publishing and networking. Knowing that I had mindfully crafted an approach helped me keep moving forward with the mindset that if I invested my energy in logical places and took a few chances when unique opportunities arose, it would pay off."

- **Second, believe in yourself and in your business.** Have faith! Trinda Latherow writes, "Before anything can come of our efforts, we must believe or know in our heart and mind that our product or service is worthwhile, useful for the betterment of others, or truly meant to be. It is our belief in self and in whatever we put out there that inspires us to persevere when all else tells us otherwise. We overcome fear with faith in self and whatever we help to create. It is that confidence that draws others to us."

- **Third, take small steps until you are ready to go all-out.** You don't have to quit your job and launch your business overnight. Take time to study other businesses, freelance, build up your skills, and ask advice from others who have been where you want to go. David Pitlyuk, founder of Carbon Fiber Gear, writes, "The way that I was able to somewhat offset my fear was by doing my business on the side for as long as I could while also working during the day. This meant a lot of late nights and busy weekends, but it allowed me to have a decent enough amount of revenue coming in so that by the time I left my job, my financial risk was much lower."

*continued on next page…*

*...continued from previous page*

- **Fourth, get support from other people.** Photographer Oana Hogrefe writes, "Have your family's support. They will have to share you with your business in different ways than they used to share you with your corporate job, so it needs to be a pursuit that makes sense to them as well."

  Sharron Jones, owner of the E-Marketing firm ShazzCo adds, "I was terrified to tell contacts about my new business in case it failed and I had to return, hat in hand, to look for a job in six months. In retrospect, it was a mistake. I could have used my network to build my client list far faster and become more profitable sooner if I hadn't been afraid that my existing contacts would snicker up their sleeves at my business idea. My advice is: Once you've decided to start your business, get the word out as quickly as possible to your entire network."

- **Fifth, look at your fears rationally.** What is the worst that can happen? Carrie Hensel, Managing Partner of Inner Circle Media, writes, "I wrote down exactly what failure meant to me. Failure meant I would have to go back to work for another company, at least for the time being. It didn't mean I was going to be destitute and alone."

  Similarly, Adam Kruse of the Hermann London Group, at www. hermannlondon.com/adam-kruse, advises, "Just do it. If you fail, you can go back to the same rut you are in now."

  Finally, Kristy Peters, Owner and Chief Artist of Lani Designs, shares that she built up the courage to make the leap by comparing the negatives of staying where she was to what was driving her to start her business: "I was okay with the risk because the alternative of staying in a desk job seemed worse. I envisioned all the scenarios if I did not start my business. I envisioned the financial scenario, the mental scenario, and how I might feel about the decision one month, one year and one decade from now...In addition, I looked at what was driving me to want to start my own business. For me it was simple: I wanted mobility and flexibility. I focused on that drive and leaned on it for support. It was the reminder I needed to keep me going forward."

- **Sixth, take action, even small action, and good things will probably start to happen.** Piano teacher and blogger Matthew McLaughlin of pianoblog.com writes, "I did have a business plan, but more importantly I did something. Worrying about infinite possible negative outcomes would have been paralyzing. Working with my strengths and learning as I went was what pulled me through. I've found that moving in one direction, even the wrong one temporarily, is almost always better than trying to think out every possible scenario in advance. Work with what you know instead of worrying about what you don't."

## MINDSET THREE: BE OPEN TO ADVICE AND HELP.

There is an old saying, paraphrased here: "Fools repeat their mistakes. Smart people learn from their mistakes. Wise people learn from the mistakes of others."

I can't name a single thriving business that ever succeeded without expertise, advice, wisdom, and help from people in addition to the founder. Whether you are shy, don't feel comfortable sharing your problems with other people, are fiercely independent, or are proud, it still is invaluable to seek out advice and help from people who have been where you are now.

Seek out other successful people before you launch your business. Test your ideas with them. Invite them to share their experiences. Ask about other people they know who might be able to help. Truly successful people are usually generous about sharing their knowledge, contacts, and even resources—and many of them have soft spots for first-time entrepreneurs.

The benefits are enormous. You avoid mistakes. You get new ideas about how to make your business succeed. You build relationships with mentors who can open up all sorts of new possibilities for you. You might even find an investor, customer, or someone who wants to buy your business in the future.

You just have to ask and be open to the advice you receive.

## MINDSET FOUR: BE ON THE LOOKOUT FOR OPPORTUNITIES.

Entrepreneurs have a wonderful knack for identifying and taking advantage of money-making opportunities. These opportunities bring value to others, while giving the entrepreneur something valuable in return. For entrepreneurs, seeing opportunities and new ways to provide value to others is a permanent filter that we use. Just as baseball scouts search for the next pitcher who can throw a 95-mile-per-hour fastball, just as movie producers search for the next *Star Wars*, so entrepreneurs constantly look for additional ways to make money while bringing value to others.

The opportunity can be ground-breaking, like inventing something along the lines of the iPhone, Google, or Tivo...but it doesn't have to be. It also can be something simple that the entrepreneur does well, or something that fills an underserved niche, such as starting a landscaping service in a growing town, or bringing a hot dog stand to a town center that only has burger joints. It can be an opportunity to help the company grow, like negotiating a deal with a distribution partner, buying remnant advertising space for a song, buying a foreclosed office building at pennies on the dollar, or starting a new service or product line based on suggestions from customers. It also can be the opportunity to hire a crack salesperson from a competitor or raise funds from an angel investor.

The entrepreneur is always on the lookout for big and small opportunities. Once he finds a potential opportunity, he answers key questions to assess its viability:

- What problem does this opportunity solve, and for whom?
- How much value does this opportunity bring to others?
- How do I make money with this opportunity?
- What other value besides money do I receive from this opportunity?
- How big can this opportunity get?
- What is required to turn this opportunity into reality?
- What information do I need to negotiate successfully with others involved in this opportunity, and how do I gain an edge?
- What can go wrong, and how do I protect myself?
- How can I use other people's resources to spread my risk?

Here is a test to see how well you embrace the mindset of seeking opportunities: Think of someone you know who happens to be an incredible expert on some topic or in a particular field—for instance, legal issues, a sport, music, technology, health, nutrition, meditation, graphic design, or public speaking. Come up with at least one way you can approach this person and develop an opportunity to make money with him or her.

For example, I know a very successful nursing executive. She has worked in dozens of healthcare systems, helping to turn them around and improve quality, service, and productivity. She is passionate about the importance of nurse managers in health systems. To her, they are the backbone of a good hospital. While we were talking one time, she shared that she was sad about how little time and money hospitals budgeted for training and developing current and up-and-coming nurse managers. Based on that conversation, I asked her if she would be interested in developing a training program with me to address that problem. She agreed, and we worked together to develop The Nurse Manager's Performance Leadership System, at healthcareperformanceinstitute.com. The program includes a manual, set of audio lectures, and ongoing support by email, all set up to train nurse managers to be more effective leaders. Health systems from around the world have bought this program. Almost everyone you know knows something, and that alone is a nearly unlimited source of opportunity for you, if you have the right mindset.

How well would you say that you identify opportunities, especially when others don't?

## MINDSET FIVE: TOLERATE IMPERFECTION.

Entrepreneurs are not perfectionists. They can't afford to be. Rather, they are okay with at least three kinds of imperfection.

First, they test new ideas in the marketplace, even if they aren't perfect yet. For instance, software and online service providers often roll out a beta test of their software, recruit a few customers to try it for low or no cost, and improve the software based on user feedback. They keep tweaking and rolling out new versions in order to respond to customer demand and still be out in the marketplace.

Similarly, rather than obsess about creating the perfect marketing campaign, entrepreneurs test and tweak. They wouldn't send out a 100,000-piece mailing that they've worked months to perfect, but they would mail 1,000 letters. If response is profitable, they will expand the mailing to another 10,000 people; they might also test a second letter at the same time to see if they can beat response from the first one. If an initial test campaign fails to get good enough results, the entrepreneur might change the offer, or some other significant element of the campaign, and test the new version. They keep testing and tweaking until they achieve success. Insisting on perfection before doing anything would paralyze the whole process, because there is never enough information to know for sure what will work without testing.

Compare this to my experience as an employee at a large consumer marketing company. If I wanted to recommend a marketing campaign, I had to write a one-page memo to my boss. He then edited it and passed it back to me for a rewrite. I rewrote it until my boss was satisfied. Then he passed the memo up to his boss, who rewrote it and passed it back down to my boss. My boss passed it back down to me, and I had to rewrite it until both my boss and his boss were satisfied—which sometimes took weeks. Finally, the memo was sent up to the company CEO, who often made his own comments, which led to a whole new round of writing and rewriting. We spent countless hours trying to read the mind of the CEO and anticipate his thoughts. No memo went to him until we felt it was perfect. Every associate at that company had a never-ending stack of memos in his inbox that needed writing and rewriting, prior to weeks of additional rewriting.

As an entrepreneur, you don't have the time to perfect a one-page memo. You have to spend your time testing, tweaking, and refining your products and marketing campaigns, all in the real world. Of course, you can't be impulsive and put out junk. However, you can't afford to obsess until every single detail is perfect, including things that your customers won't notice. At some point, you have to launch the best product or service you can to a limited audience, with the resources you have. Once you get feedback based on real behavior from real consumers, use that information to tweak and improve.

The second form of imperfection that you have to live with as an entrepreneur is incomplete knowledge. You can't know everything it takes to get a business started, and yet you have to take action. I resisted this fact of life for a long time, and this resistance delayed my goal of starting a business. In my case, many aspects of running a business were complete mysteries to me. How did you design a logo? How did you incorporate? What was a purchase order? Where did I go to get products produced? I figured that I had to go to business school, and then work in different companies and functions for years and years in order to learn how to do all of these things. What a mistake! All I had to do was find people who did know, and either hire them or ask them for advice. You don't have to know every minute detail about how your car's ignition switch works in order to put your key in the ignition and start up your car, and you don't have to know every logistical detail of running a business in order to get started as an entrepreneur.

Similarly, entrepreneurs understand that we rarely get to have all of the information we would like to have in order to make a decision. Most of the time, we feel lucky if we have even sixty percent of the information we need to decide on a strategy or course of action. We don't have the luxury of expensive focus groups and market research studies. We have to find creative ways to get information and collect data. Once we have a fair percentage of the information we would like, we make a decision. Then we take action as appropriate, measure results, learn, and improve from there.

Information gathering gets easier and more precise as the business grows. For instance, when you first start out, you may not know exactly where your best marketing investment will be. However, because you track and measure the results of every single dollar you invest in marketing, your knowledge about your most profitable marketing tactics grows over time. You also learn more about customer loyalty, customer needs, what makes a great employee, and where the market is heading.

Third, and perhaps most challenging for the entrepreneur, you can't expect perfect, instant market acceptance as soon as you roll out your first product or marketing campaign. For instance, a stay-at-home-mom recently launched a website in order to generate additional income for her family. She spent two weeks creating the site, setting up the advertising, writing her first few blogs, and telling everyone she knew to visit and to tell their friends about it. After two weeks, when traffic didn't magically reach thousands of visitors, she decided to give up. She expected an overnight success and wasn't willing to keep fighting when her expectations weren't met. She needed to understand that, despite occasional news stories about instantly viral websites and videos, immediate success is rare. In our imperfect world—where it takes time to get visible, build credibility, and establish trust—the entrepreneur has to be prepared mentally to keeping going and not give up.

Taken together, the three types of imperfection require the entrepreneur to build the house as he lives in it. While he builds, he learns. He might tear down a wall, change the paint colors, and put up a different front door than he first planned. He might discover that the foundation is a bit crooked and jack up the house to make it level. As he gets more comfortable in the house and has more money to spend, he might add a room or two, and maybe put in a pool out back. He keeps improving the house as he goes, based on first-hand experience and information. What he doesn't do is invest all of his money to design and build the perfect house, only to move in and find that the house is worth very little on the market.

Take a moment to consider this mindset. Be sure that you are okay launching a business before everything is perfect. Be sure you are okay building the house while you live in it. If you need to wait for perfection, your business might never get off the ground.

## MINDSET SIX: IMPROVISE WITH FINESSE, ESPECIALLY IN THE FACE OF LIMITED RESOURCES.

Entrepreneurs are master improvisers. They have no choice, because without unlimited resources, they have to figure out creative ways to keep the business running.

The crux of improvisational acting is the "Yes, and…" game. In this game, you take something that someone else says, and—no matter how crazy it is—you say yes to it and build on it. This game teaches you to accept what is, to be open to new ideas without shooting them down, and to come up with creative solutions. For instance, suppose that a potential client tells you that your prices are too high, and you really want their business. Come up with a few sentences that start with "Yes, and…" to make the sale anyway. For instance:

- Yes, and I was only kidding about those prices.
- Yes, and I forgot to tell you about all of the extra products and support you get with these prices.
- Yes, and if you order this week I can give you a discount that will work for you.
- Yes, and if you pay up front instead of using the installment plan that I built into this price, I can reduce your price significantly.

- Yes, and if you agree to this price, I can offer you an interest-free payment plan to stretch your payments over time.
- Yes, and if you increase the size of your order, you can pay a lot less per item.
- Yes, and if you reduce the scope of the project, you can pay a lot less.
- Yes, and if you agree to give me five referrals to other potential clients, I can give you a great discount on price.

Following are a few other situations to challenge your ability to improvise:

- How can you get office or warehouse space that is outside your home, for free? One entrepreneur found a new office building that was empty. He convinced the landlord to give him space for pennies on the dollar; the landlord agreed because he wanted to show that he had some tenants. Another entrepreneur found a warehouse space that was half full and convinced the business owner who was renting the space to let him use it for free while he got his business up and running.
- How can you get a free endorsement from a well-known professional athlete or celebrity? The answer: Ask! You never know what the response will be. I got a Hall of Fame football player to write a testimonial for one of my books simply by asking. He read the book, liked it, and wrote a glowing testimonial for me.
- How can you meet the most influential person in your town and get his or her support for your business? Many entrepreneurs have a knack for meeting influential people. If you are just starting out, one of the best ways to meet influential people is by calling them and asking them for advice. In general, successful people like to mentor others who are getting started. Who knows? You might find a lifelong mentor who can help you make important connections and avoid mistakes.
- What is one way to get great exposure for your business, without spending a dime? There are many ways to get free exposure. You could become a member of an important committee in town, like the economic development committee at your Chamber of Commerce. You could get involved at a leadership level in planning a major community event, like a fundraiser for a non-profit or a holiday parade. Or come

up with your own charity event and get other businesses to join you in sponsoring it. Finally, you can always do something creative that gets you noticed, like the hot dog entrepreneur who ran a marathon in a hot dog costume.

- How can you get your products or services featured on television without paying an expensive publicist? The answer is that you pick up the phone and pitch a story that the station's viewers will like. One entrepreneur started by pitching her story to a small local television station, who interviewed her for a segment. Then she pitched her knowledge to big city stations. Now she makes regular appearances on national morning shows.

- How can you form a joint marketing partnership with one of the largest businesses in your area? If you can find a way to provide value, you can get other businesses to partner with you. For instance, find businesses whose products complement yours and work together in order to offer one-stop service to customers. If you run a mortgage business, you can team up with a title company, a real estate brokerage, and a moving company to form an alliance that offers everything a customer needs to sell their home and buy another.

- A potential customer challenges you, "What qualifies you to offer this service?" How do you respond if this is your first customer? It's simple. Look the customer in the eye and say, "I am among the best in this business, and I personally guarantee that you are going to be delighted with the results and service I provide. I can make this guarantee with confidence because I have the training and the drive, and because—based on our conversations—I would really enjoy working with you."

- How can you get 20 testimonials for your business immediately, before you have even opened your doors? First, you can ask twenty friends, colleagues, and former classmates to write a testimonial attesting to your character and ethics; they may not be able to write about your current business, but they can testify about you. Second, give a speech at a local Chamber of Commerce or Rotary and ask people to write down one thing that they found valuable in your speech, as well as for their permission for you to use their comment in your marketing materials. After your speech, you will have some great testimonials from almost everyone who heard you speak.

- How can you get someone to design your logo and marketing materials for you at little or no cost to you? Nike is famous for having its swoosh logo designed by a student. You can do the same. Many graphic design students are hungry to build their portfolios, and many of them are quite talented. They will often give you a discounted rate in exchange for a testimonial or reference.

- How can you get your website up without spending more than a couple hundred dollars and without going to the trouble of doing it yourself? I use Elance.com to find low-cost, highly talented web designers from around the world. One designer in India does top-notch work for me at extremely reasonable prices.

- How can you create the impression that your business is large and established when you are the only one working there? An entrepreneur who ran a two-person software development company faced this problem every time potential customers and investors came to his office to check out his business. He would get his friends to bring their laptops to his office and pretend to be employees while these VIPs visited. When he couldn't recruit enough friends, he hired some temporary workers to fill seats in the office. Eventually he sold his company for around $3 million. You can also set up an extensive voice mail system with a number of extensions so that your business seems bigger than it is, or at least hire a virtual assistant to answer the phone for you.

- A prospective client says no to the million-dollar consulting project you have proposed. How can you still keep the door open to getting business from them? Whenever a prospective client rejects my big proposal, I suggest that they start with a low-cost diagnostic or assessment. That way, they can test me out and see my value at a low cost, while I continue to nurture the relationship and show them what I can do for them.

Warning: There is a fine line between improvising, finessing, and downright lying. You have to make your own determination about when you are crossing the line into sleazy or unethical territory. However, don't become a victim and tell yourself, "I can't start a business because it's impossible to start a business without being unethical." There are always creative ways that don't cross the line to move your business forward with few or no resources. Keep developing your ability to improvise and finesse while being honest, and you will see that this is true.

# MINDSET SEVEN: MINIMIZE DOWNSIDE RISK WHILE MAXIMIZING YOUR UPSIDE.

True entrepreneurs don't blow their personal savings on a dream and a prayer. They are masters at minimizing their risks while maximizing their upside. They use other people's money to get the venture going, or they start businesses that they can bootstrap with very little investment capital. In my own case, I always set a stop loss before going into a business. If I see that I am going to spend more than the stop loss I have set, I close down the business rather than waste another dime. Right now my stop loss is $2,500, and I only invest in business opportunities where I believe that I can make 100 times that amount.

Many entrepreneurs won't even start a new business unless they already know they will succeed, for example, by having at least a few customers ready to buy. They follow military strategist Sun Tzu's advice never to fight a battle unless they are sure they will win.

Here are some case studies to test your ability to manage risk. Assuming that you face the situations that follow, how would you minimize your risk and maximize your upside?

- **Case #1: Self-publish a book without spending a dime or even doing more than a little bit of writing.** Thanks to digital presses like Lulu.com and the Internet, you can publish a book and keep 90% of the proceeds. However, you have to be smart about how you do it. One way to reduce your risk is to get a group of experts to all agree to write a chapter of the book, and pay their share of the costs of getting the book published. You can be the editor and write an introduction and conclusion. In other words, for almost no money and very little work, you can get your book published, be the main expert, and have other people market the book to their list on your behalf.

- **Case #2: You have run out of cash for your business and have to dip into your personal savings, including your retirement funds, to keep the business going. What do you do to minimize risk and maximize upside?** If your business runs out of cash, you have a flaw in your business model or in your planning process. Until you can bring in more cash than goes out, you also have a hobby instead of a viable business. At this point, you have a few options. First, shut down the business and find a real source of income. Alternatively, take what you have learned so far from the business and tweak the business model so that it will succeed going forward. However, this time get an investor to fund the business; if you can't convince an investor, then consider the possibility that your business still doesn't have legs. Third, if you can't get an investor, commit to bootstrapping the business creatively so that you don't spend another dime of your own money to get it up and running.

- **Case #3: You are sick and tired of working as a manager for a national consumer finance company. You want to start up your own consumer finance business. How can you do this with absolutely no risk to you?** The entrepreneur in this situation did a few things. First, he set up shop in the basement of his home to keep overhead to a minimum. Second, he started prospecting for customers at night and on weekends, and only left his job after he had tested and refined his selling system and had five customers ready to buy from him. Third, he hired away the two best salespeople he knew in the industry and put them on a generous commission schedule so that they could make far more than they ever did at their previous employer. Meanwhile, he paid commission only, so that he had no ongoing salary expenses. With this strategy, the entrepreneur built up a multi-million dollar business within a year of starting out on his own.

## MINDSET EIGHT: INFLUENCE OTHERS.

One important attribute of the entrepreneur is the ability to influence others. We are always on the lookout for opportunities to make requests and persuade others to think, speak, feel, or act in ways that support their own goals. We do this by figuring out what the other person wants and then crafting a way for everyone to win.

If you want to build your ability to influence others, practice in daily situations. For instance, try to negotiate a free appetizer or dessert at a restaurant. Get yourself upgraded to first class even if you don't have the miles or frequent flyer status. Go to a bank and ask for a $25,000 collateral-free loan. Convince an influential person in your town to be a mentor to you.

Before you try to influence the other person, take the time to come up with a strategy. What reasons can you offer them to agree to your request? What can you offer them in return? What questions can you ask them to understand what they want, and then come up with a win-win deal?

If people say no to you, take responsibility for the result you got without blaming the other person or yourself. Take a step back and reassess the approach you took. How can you change your tactics next time in order to achieve your goal? Alternatively, move on to other goals. Always be influencing!

## MINDSET NINE: DEVELOP THICK SKIN.

Don't take setbacks personally or care about looking foolish while you get your business up and running. The people around you have preconceived notions about who you are and what your potential is. If you haven't started a business before, many of them might not believe that you will succeed. At the same time, many people project their own insecurity and jealousy onto others who seem to be living the life that they want to live. In other words, expect lots of people to pass negative judgment on you when you decide to go out on your own.

At the same time, expect many, many setbacks when you run your business. Your first partner when you start up a business is named Murphy, and his notorious laws will test your resolve every single day. Customers won't pay. Suppliers won't ship on time, or they will ship defective products. Government bureaucrats will hold up your progress and take more taxes and fees than you ever expected. Your computers will crash. You will try a few marketing campaigns that fail miserably. It will take longer than you ever thought to get your first customer. Your bank account will come perilously close to zero.

You have to thicken your skin if you want to make the leap from employee to entrepreneur. Before you jump, make sure you can handle scenarios like these:

- Your parents tell you that your business idea is stupid and that you will fail.

- Your significant other laughs at you when you present your idea. Worse, they threaten to leave you if you give up your job.

- During your first year in business, you make no salary and barely cover your living expenses. Your second year, you make a quarter of your previous salary.

- You realize that you can't eat out anymore, take long vacations, or hang out as much with your friends while you get the business going.

- Your friends stop calling you because you keep turning them down while they go out and have a great time—all while you work on your business.

Here is a great exercise to do right now in order to find out if you have the thick skin required to be an entrepreneur: Go out right now, find 20 people, and make a request of each one, with the goal of having them say, "No." Ask for a free sandwich at a deli. Ask a cab driver to drive you around town for free. Ask a complete stranger for a dollar; if he says yes, ask him for ten dollars instead. Don't ask for things that will get you arrested or punched out. Simply ask for things and see what happens. Make it your mission to have people say no to you. If you get comfortable with this exercise and do it every day, you will get over any issues you have about being rejected or looking foolish promoting your business.

## MINDSET TEN: KEEP MOVING FORWARD, NO MATTER HOW LOUSY YOU FEEL AT THE MOMENT.

As I finished writing the last paragraph, on a rainy Tuesday afternoon, my wife called to ask me to go to a matinee movie with her and the kids. I would much rather spend time with my family than write. But I have set a deadline to complete this book, and I reserved this block of time to write. I want to go to the movie; however, I know that I have to keep pressing forward and on schedule. Occasionally I'll spontaneously close the office and be with my family in the middle of a workday, but today is not one of those days.

Entrepreneurs wake up every morning and have to make a choice: Move the business forward, or let it slip back. Some mornings we feel lazy, tired, burned out, and depressed. Still, we get up and do what we need to do to keep the business on track.

Our immediate impulses are fleeting and distracting. You can't let them get in the way of achieving your goals or weaken your resolve to make things happen. You have to have the internal drive and inspiration to set the example and keep moving forward. If you don't, who will?

Employees can call in sick and go fishing. Serious entrepreneurs can't and won't—especially when they are just getting started. Yes, you can take time out to recharge. But please don't start a business if you don't have the resolve to make things happen, regardless of how you feel at the moment.

# MINDSET ELEVEN: THINK CRITICALLY ABOUT THE BUSINESS, WITHOUT DRINKING THE KOOL-AID.

You are passionate about your business and have thick skin when others say negative things. However, this doesn't make it smart to ignore the facts. You have to think critically about the business, interpret data correctly, and listen to other experts when they give you qualified advice. For instance:

- Suppose that an investor gives you tough feedback about your business model and makes a compelling case about why your business plan is flawed. Do you shrug his opinion off and look for other investors, or do you listen and consider the possibility that his advice is sound? Like it or not, other people might have important insights about ways for you to improve your business. Some people might just like to dump on you to hide their own jealousy, but others will see things that you missed. Be open to their advice. I know that in my own case, I rejected the advice of a few potential investors about one of my business plans, and it turned out that they were right. I could have saved a lot of money if I had listened.

- It is time to reorder the first product your business launched. You love this product, and it has lots of meaning to you because it was the first product you ever designed, produced, and marketed. Unfortunately, this product isn't a big seller anymore. The $3,000 in cash required to place a minimum order would represent about three years of inventory that you have to store. You could use the $3,000 on other, potentially more profitable products and strategies. On the other hand, you would feel terrible having to take this product off your website. What should you do? This case is a very real, very poignant example of the choice one entrepreneur had to make. As an objective outsider, my advice would be for the entrepreneur to get rid of the product and focus on other, more lucrative opportunities. Unfortunately, the entrepreneur couldn't let the product die a dignified death. She paid $3,000 to buy more, admitting that she was acting out of pure emotion. The product still sits in her storage unit, unsold.

- Your partner in the business is not carrying his weight. However, he is your best friend since kindergarten. What do you do? The answer is that you separate the business from your friendship. Partners in a business need to do their share. Have a collegial discussion with the partner to understand why he isn't carrying his weight and whether he has the same perceptions as you. Communicate your expectations and work out an agreement for how you will measure mutual performance going forward. If the partner continues to disappoint, buy him out or have him take a lesser share of the business.

- You thought you had a great business strategy. Unfortunately, you are now $75,000 in debt trying to keep the business going—which is $10,000 more than the limit you set for investing your own money. Your credit cards are maxed out, and you have drained your retirement savings. Your last option is to max out your home equity line of credit. You love your business, especially the glamour, the freedom, and the press coverage. People in the community have come to know your business and respect you. You don't want to let go, no matter how scared and upset your wife and kids are. You figure that if you keep at it, soon you will attract enough customers to be profitable. What do you do?

In my judgment, this person never should have let the business cost more than the limit that he set. The purpose of a business is to make you money. In this case, the so-called entrepreneur is paying other people for glamour and respect, while his family suffers. He should either get other people to invest in the business—which seems unlikely based on the few facts presented—or close it down and cut his losses before he loses his house and puts his family at risk of facing complete financial ruin. He is drinking the Kool-Aid. Make sure that you don't.

# MINDSET TWELVE: TAKE 100 PERCENT RESPONSIBILITY.

When you run a business, there is nowhere to hide. You are 100 percent responsible for every result you get or don't get—without excuses, blaming, or obsessing about what could have been. If an employee doesn't do something right, you have to make sure that he has the support and training to do it right next time. If he still gets it wrong, you have to find someone who can do it right.

Similarly, suppose that your employees tell you that they feel like they have to read your mind in order to know your expectations. It would not be especially effective to take their feedback personally and snap back at them. Taking responsibility means that you listen to what they have to say and that, if it makes sense for your success and the success of the business, you change your behavior.

What if you try to influence a vendor to work overtime to get you an order, and he refuses? You can yell, scream, and threaten—and in some cases, that might work…once. Taking responsibility in this situation means looking at why you needed the order rushed, and then fixing your processes to place orders in a timely manner. It also means working with your vendors to make it worth their while to rush orders for you in certain circumstances.

How about if someone writes a bad review of your products or services? Do you threaten a lawsuit? Do you argue against the review—which will only draw more attention to the negative review and make you look like a whiner?

Instead, evaluate the review, improve your products and services, and invite the reviewer back to test out your changes. Let the public know that you listened and made improvements. Domino's Pizza did that by demolishing their old pizza recipe and coming up with a completely new one, and the initial results seem to be positive.

Customer complaints, defective shipments, late payments, poor hiring choices, accounting errors, and slow weeks are all part of business. Don't take them personally. Don't blame. Take responsibility by looking at the result you got, why you got it, and how you can get a better result next time. If you don't have the mindset to approach setbacks this way, you shouldn't go into business for yourself.

Take the following assessment to identify which of these twelve mindsets are strengths for you, and which ones you have to develop.

## ASSESSMENT: HAVE YOU WON THE MENTAL BATTLE?

| Mindset | Strong | So-So | Weak |
|---|---|---|---|
| One: Get rid of any misperceptions about owning a business. | | | |
| Two: I can do this. | | | |
| Three: Be open to advice and help. | | | |
| Four: See lucrative opportunities when others don't. | | | |
| Five: Tolerate imperfection. | | | |
| Six: Improvise with finesse, especially in the face of limited resources. | | | |
| Seven: Minimize risk and downside while maximizing upside. | | | |
| Eight: Influence others. | | | |
| Nine: Develop thick skin. | | | |
| Ten: Keep moving forward, regardless of how you feel at the moment. | | | |
| Eleven: Think critically about the business, without drinking the Kool-Aid. | | | |
| Twelve: Take 100 percent responsibility. | | | |

# ONE OF THE MOST INSPIRING BUSINESS QUOTES EVER...
## Remember It Any Time You Need to Get into the Right Mindset:

If you have never read William H. Murray's inspiring and famous quote from his *The Scottish Himalayan Expedition* (1951), you need to. Once you read it, you will want to write it down and put it somewhere you can read it whenever you need inspiration. To respect copyright laws, please visit www.JobEscapePlan.com for a link to this quote.

## Chapter Two

# BATTLE NUMBER TWO:
## Come Up with a Workable Idea

A business needs a good idea to start. Fortunately, your idea doesn't need to be earth-shattering, and there are almost unlimited places you can go to come up with a workable business idea. This chapter provides you with a partial reference guide of sources where you can get ideas to start your business.

---

### WARNING: SCAM ALERT

While coming up with your business idea, be cautious. Watch out for so-called business opportunities that are scams in disguise, or at least questionable. Many people fall for dubious business opportunities, because they are gullible, desperate, or really want to be part of an organization that appears to be exciting. Do your due diligence before you sign up for any kind of business opportunity! Sometimes the best decision you can make in business is to say no.

For instance, don't fall prey to work at home scams that require payment up front for you to buy in. Watch out for multi-level marketing schemes where you aren't one of the very first people at the very top level and where the person above you doesn't have a track record of making serious money in multi-level marketing businesses. Avoid franchises that: don't have a recognized, trusted brand; don't have a large number of profitable, long-term franchisees; and that won't let you talk to former franchisees that have dropped out of the system.

Also, be on guard for high-energy group meetings that sell you on joining the business. Often these meetings are filled with shills who pretend to show interest in buying into the business. The shills are there to create social proof. If a few people show interest in an idea, others are more likely to take notice and want to get involved—while the shills get paid a generous commission in return for their infectious enthusiasm.

*...continued on next page*

---

---

*...continued from previous page*

Another area filled with scam artists is the invention consulting business. I know, because when I was in college I paid a few hundred dollars to one of these firms to help me bring an invention idea of mine to market. First they gave me a free consulting session, where they told me my idea had potential. Then I paid them for a consulting report, which produced a very generic overview of my invention and its pros and cons. After I got the report, a slick salesman tried to persuade me to pay lots more money for them to help protect my idea and market it. At that point, I had enough. Looking back, I'm embarrassed to admit that I paid even a penny to this firm and mention the issue only to keep you from making the same mistake.

Finally, watch out for get-wealthy products sold on late-night infomercials and at free seminars. If no-money-down real estate, day-trading software, and the cash flow businesses were so lucrative, these so-called experts would not be sharing their proprietary secrets with strangers like you!

---

As you read through the following list of sources for business ideas, challenge yourself to come up at least five ideas that might be worthwhile to explore further. Write them down, whether you think they are good or bad. The key is to get your creative juices flowing and to be able to generate business opportunities as a habit. For each idea you write down, commit to taking one action step this week to assess the idea and refine it.

Sources of ideas:

**Start with where you are now and where you have been: your experiences, talents, and contacts.** Often the best idea is right in front of you, and you might not even know it. For instance, a participant in my Certified Executive Coach training program was trying to choose a target market for his coaching practice. He came up with all sorts of ideas that had very little to do with his background but seemed glamorous and exciting to him. Then, almost as an aside, he mentioned that he was spending the weekend teaching a university course to foreign executives about advanced English for conducting negotiations and demonstrating proper business protocol. I asked him whether coaching multi-national executives about protocol, negotiations, and cultural sensitivity might be a lucrative coaching practice for him. After we played around with the idea for a while he said, "I can't believe it. It was right there in front of me the whole time and I didn't see it." Now he is building a business focused on that area and enjoying solid results.

Similarly, Wendy Piersall, founder of the mom blog network Woo! Jr., originally ran a network of business blogs. She had considered starting up a network of blogs for moms and kids, but she didn't think there would be money in that. "I wanted to be an important business woman, not a mom blogger," she said. Eventually she started a blog for moms and kids anyway, and it took off. In six months she was making more money in blogs for moms than she did with her business blog network. "I'm a mom, and I should have seen the value in that," she explains. Again, the idea was right there in front of her; she only had to accept it.

The same principle applies in my own career. I've wasted countless hours and dollars dreaming up product ideas that had nothing to do with my expertise, contacts, or ability to execute: toys, fads along the lines of the Pet Rock, inventions, and even a professional sports league. In the end, my most lucrative businesses have been based on doing what I have always done best, ever since I was a student: researching and writing.

Many people spend their whole lives looking for some kind of magical idea, an amazing invention, change-the-world service, or online business that has never been done before. They are like Ralph Kramden and Ed Norton on the classic television show *The Honeymooners*. These two guys constantly came up with crazy ideas that they had no competence to develop, and that got them into all sorts of trouble. Their antics make classic television comedy but also provide a cautionary tale for anyone looking for business ideas. By identifying your actual experiences and talents instead of focusing on ideas far outside your expertise, you are much more likely to come up with a seriously profitable business idea.

If you've worked as a plumber, start a business that has something to do with plumbing. If you are an elementary school teacher, develop products that parents of elementary school kids will buy. If you work as a veterinary assistant, come up with a product or service that pet owners need. If you coach kids' baseball on weekends, develop a product or service that helps kids play better baseball. If you work for a pool design and construction company, start a business that provides services to pool owners.

One reason so many people start a business in their forties is because they have had at least twenty years of work experience. They know an industry well. They understand distribution, operations, and marketing. They know people with crucial talents and experience. All they have to do is take what they already know and turn it into their own business.

While you don't have to be in your forties to start a business, it is true that your best idea might be right in front of your eyes! What are your skills and talents? What kinds of results can you get that other people value? Answer those questions, and you probably have your best business idea.

> *When deciding to start a new business, the closer you stick to what you know—the expertise or skill set that makes you good at your current job—the better your chances of success. The learning curve is extremely steep as a first-time entrepreneur; you want to be sure that you already know plenty about the industry and what it will take to be successful.*
>
> **—Eric Golden**, President, Equipois Inc.

**Build on a passion or hobby.** What gets you so excited and passionate that you could do it all the time? If you can find a way to make money with this passion, you can convert it into a business. Jaden Hair of www.steamykitchen.com started her profitable Asian Cooking business out of a passion for teaching people Asian cooking. She created a blog as a way to store family recipes online, and that blog exploded into a profitable business once she started accepting advertisements.

My friend and tennis coach Steve Martin—not the comedian—has a passion and a talent for identifying growth stocks. He has taken this passion and created a newsletter, www.fitstocks.com, to help other investors develop healthy and smart investing habits.

While passion seems like an obvious source for a business idea, it takes some creativity and work to turn a passion into a business. The promise in Marsha Sinetar's book title, *Do What You Love and the Money Will Follow,* is only partly true. To turn a passion into a business, you have to shift from doing what you love to the hard work of attracting customers and making a profit. There is a lot of mundane work involved in starting and running a business, work that might drain your passion. For instance, many people who love to cook have started a restaurant and lost everything; they were unable to translate their passion for cooking into a going concern because they didn't take into account all of the other things that go into running a successful restaurant besides cooking for family and friends.

Still, you never know. If you can overcome the challenges required to convert a hobby or passion into a business, you will have the inspiration and drive required to keep going while your business becomes profitable.

---

# CASE STUDY:
## George Zaharoff—A Passion for Fashion
## Overcomes Devastating Business Setbacks

George Zaharoff knew he wanted to be in fashion since he was eight years old. In high school, he even wrote letters to John Nordstrom, founder of the Nordstrom chain, telling him he wanted to get into fashion. Nordstrom wrote back, "Keep your dream."

After college, he went to Milan to try to break into fashion with his own line. He fell flat on his face. "I had the best clothes, but no infrastructure to compete. It was too big for me."

His father told him, "You need to find a job."

George replied, "The thing I want to do is fashion."

At age 22, he went to Nordstrom with a prototype for a perfume, and the retailer bought it. He grew his business in just a few years to $3 million in wholesale revenues and a line of 10 different products in 100 stores.

At that point, a major fashion house offered to buy and fund his fragrance business. The deal was scheduled to close on September 11, 2001. Before the deal, George started making the transition, letting his staff go and shifting production to the acquiring company. He also spent some of the money he expected to get from the sale of his company. When 9/11 happened, the company called the deal off.

George lost everything and had to file bankruptcy. He remembers, "It took me a good six months to get my butt out of bed and figure out what to do with myself. Everyone knew what had happened to me. People didn't return my calls. Relatives came up to me and told me, 'I knew you'd never succeed.'"

Nine months later, another leading fashion house offered to back him, if he could get all of his previous stores back on board to buy his products. He logged 400,000 frequent flyer points flying back and forth to pull things together. Once again, at the last minute, due to the war in Iraq and a bad economy, this company also put the deal on hold, and he lost everything again.

*continued on next page...*

---

*...continued from previous page*

After the setback, his father repeated, "When are you going to get it through your head that your dream is dead? You have to do something else."

He replied, "Dad, I want to do this."

An executive at Nordstrom who had supported George all along called him into his office. "You need one break," he told him. "I am going to give that break to you." He made a call to one of the biggest clothing brand companies in the world. Within a few weeks George cut a licensing deal to sell his line of men's suits with that company. Within two weeks he was back in business.

In 2008, the recession brought his business to a screeching halt once again. His licensing deal fell apart when the licensor went into bankruptcy.

George picked himself up yet again. This time he partnered up with an innovation strategy firm and venture investor, which provided funding for him to continue his business. He has rebuilt his business once again, with a growing number of retail accounts across the country offering his shirts, suits, neckwear, and women's collection.

Here is George's advice about handling setbacks, to any reader who wants to turn their lifelong passion into a business: "It sounds like a cliché, but never, ever, ever, ever give up. Be true to your vision. The best advice I got was from my therapist, who told me, 'Keep moving forward, and don't listen to anyone else.'"

---

**Make creative connections.** Many of the best business ideas come from entrepreneurs who make creative connections between two or more ideas or businesses. For instance, I started my career with a very profitable consumer marketing company. I couldn't stand the products that the company sold—collectible plates with pictures of wolves, porcelain heirloom dolls mass-manufactured in China, and tacky Christmas ornaments. However, the company had a brilliant system and process for testing products at low cost, rolling out successful products, and creating a list of loyal and very profitable customers. After a year I left the company and went to work for a business consulting firm. At that company, I learned how to help companies become more productive and profitable, as well as how to develop leading-edge training and professional development programs. However, I couldn't put up with the constant travel and long hours. After those experiences, I saw an opportunity to combine the best-practice marketing tactics of the first company with what I learned about coaching, consulting, and training from the second company. Now one of my businesses offers executive education programs online, merging the best of both worlds from my own unique experiences.

Here is an exercise to help you come up with creative connections: First, write down a list of your three favorite businesses in the world, whether local mom and pop companies or global corporations. Then write down what each company does best. Next, try to come up with a company that combines two or three of these things in a way that would be new and interesting. For instance, the three companies that come to my mind first are: McDonald's restaurants; a local restaurant in town where I get lobster; and the club where I play tennis. McDonald's is brilliant at providing consistently prepared food, fast. The local lobster restaurant serves tasty lobster rolls and boiled lobster. Finally, my tennis club is a great place for informal but serious tennis.

What ideas can you come up with that combine two or three of these things? Maybe there's an opportunity to create a chain of restaurants focused on lobster rolls. Or maybe someone could build a food services business that contracts with health and tennis clubs to provide consistent, healthy, fresh food to members. Perhaps someone could get both a major seafood company and McDonald's to sponsor a tennis tournament at local tennis clubs.

You can take this exercise further and really get creative. Write down three words that are either nouns, or that are verbs that end in "ing." Try to form a company around two or three of these word combinations. For example, suppose you write down: computers, banana cream pie, and dancing. What ideas for a business can you come up with? Here are some options: an online company that delivers homemade pies; a coffee shop with the best wireless service and pies in the world; an online website that rates people's ability to dance; a dance studio for computer nerds; an online cooking school that teaches people how to make great desserts; an adult education business that teaches people fun skills like baking and dancing; an online service that brings dance lessons directly to your home; a national banana pie speed eating competition; or an online service for companies looking for top dance talent for commercials and movies.

Let yourself play. See what you come up with. Don't censor your ideas. There is plenty of time for that later. For now, try to come up with at least three ideas by making creative connections.

**Market information that is concise, packaged, and solves a problem for people overwhelmed with data.** Almost everybody knows something that other people would like to know, too. Plus, people are overwhelmed with data, but none of it is organized in useful, easy-to-access ways. If you can package what you know in a convenient way, you might be able to create a lucrative business.

Take some time to list some things you know that others might value. In my own case, I've sold information packages about how to start and run a successful medical practice, how to market a fitness practice, how to market an information technology business, how to be an executive coach, how to be a business coach, how to be a career coach, how to be an image consultant, and how to be a more effective executive. My wife Elena happens to be an international expert on etiquette, and she has created a business helping people teach etiquette in their communities.

People are interested in all sorts of information: how to make more money, how to write an iPhone app, how to be healthier, how to play a sport better, how to get children to behave better, how to find a mate, how to have a happy marriage, how to cook, how to do social marketing, how to save for retirement, how to get out of debt, how to avoid getting ripped off at the car dealership, how to influence others, how to be an effective public speaker, how to speak a new language, how to travel and experience a foreign country like a local, how to fix common problems in a home, how to cure back pain, how to lower taxes, how to sleep better, and how to organize a closet. The list is almost limitless!

Write down at least one thing you know well enough to teach others. How might you take what you know and package it to others so that they can solve a pressing problem?

**Launch a low fixed-cost, easy-to-start local service business.** Your business idea doesn't have to be earth-shattering. In fact, you can create a me-too business that others already do and still be quite successful. Look around for businesses that are in demand in your area: landscaping, massage, tutoring, cleaning, catering, photography, computer repair, pest control, painting, and so many more. In these types of businesses, you have to create a marketing message that sets you apart, hustle for customers, and then provide outstanding value so that your customers keep hiring you and then rave about you to others.

**Solve nagging problems in your life.** Almost every successful company starts with the solution to a pressing problem. What are things that annoy you as you go through your day? Stop complaining and start a business around one of them. Other people probably get annoyed by those things, too, and they might pay if you can eliminate one of these problems for them. For instance, my wife created a product called The Goodnight Stop Light to keep our kids from getting out of bed at night. That product became the core of her company, which has since expanded into 46 countries with dozens of products and services. Every time you catch yourself sighing in frustration, cursing, or complaining, ask yourself if you can somehow solve the issue with a product or service that others might buy. A single product doesn't make a successful company, but it can be a good start.

**Solve nagging problems at work.** The same approach applies at your job. Which vendors might be doing a mediocre job? What equipment keeps breaking down? What kinds of services and products would make your job easier? What kinds of training programs do workers need that they are not getting? What kind of talent is in high demand? How well do the people at your company understand how to use the latest technologies? How can the company get supplies or services at lower cost than it pays now? Any of these questions can lead you to potentially solid business ideas.

**Address other people's complaints.** Don't just listen for your own complaints; listen to what others complain about, too. If you hear someone say, "I wish that…" you might have the kernel of an idea for a new company.

**Take advantage of bad service experiences when you buy from other companies.** One way to identify a good business idea is by figuring out a way to beat other companies. If you hire a company and they don't meet your expectations, start up a competitor. Is the pizza in your town lousy? Start up a better pizza joint. Are there no reliable computer repair services? Start one.

**Get on the front lines in sales.** To really learn about a market and customer preferences, get a sales job with a growing company. Before long, you will learn almost everything there is to know about the marketplace, the competition, and what customers want. With that kind of knowledge, you can identify gaps in the market and fill needs that nobody else is addressing.

**Identify opportunities in growing towns and cities.** Growing towns and cities need all sorts of services: movie theaters, restaurants, babysitting, pet sitters, taxi services, handymen, delivery services, gyms, personal trainers, real estate brokers, moving services, and on and on. If you live in a rapidly growing area, choose a service and commit to being the best at providing it. In my town, the leading local real estate firm started out in the 1970s, when most of the roads were unpaved. Now the company dominates the market, especially for waterfront and luxury homes. If you like this approach to finding business ideas but don't live in a thriving town or city, maybe you should consider moving to one.

**Follow demographic trends.** Some trends are clear and indisputable, which means that you know the future and can capitalize on it. For instance, we all know that the population is aging and people are living longer. Also, the United States population keeps getting more diverse, with rapid growth among Hispanics and Asians. Social Security is going broke, and too many people haven't planned for retirement. The current generation of workers insists on greater flexibility at work; they have also been raised on texting, social networking, and mobile applications. China and India are producing hundreds of millions—yes, hundreds of millions—of middle class workers who want to enjoy a better quality of life. These and many other trends in society present you with business opportunities. For instance, an aging population creates opportunities to provide home health care to people who don't want to go into nursing homes. The growth in the Hispanic population means that lots of companies will pay big dollars to learn how to market to Hispanics. If you can broker opportunities between China or India and the USA, teach English speakers how to do business there, or teach Chinese or Indians to do business here, you might build a thriving company. Why not ride the wave of clear demographic trends?

**Find opportunities in growing or changing industries.** Industry growth and change create opportunities. For instance, when new healthcare reimbursement rules came out in the 1980s, one entrepreneur saw that hospitals were going to go broke if they didn't change the way they did business. Starting with three partners working around a coffee table in his home office, he built a healthcare consulting firm that grew to 350 employees and $80 million in revenues. Recent healthcare reform may create similar opportunities. Meanwhile, all sorts of industries are experiencing rapid change due to the Internet, overseas competition, government intervention, environmental concern, and huge demand in emerging countries. What industry changes do you know about? What opportunities open up for you because of these changes?

**Create an idea that changes the world, or at least an industry.** The Dyson Vacuum Cleaner, FedEx, Tivo, Google, the iPhone, the iPad: all of these are ideas that have shaken up entire industries and, in some cases, changed the world. The problem with game-changing ideas is that they can take a long time and lots of money to make happen. Dyson spent years of his life and fought huge lawsuits before his unique vacuum cleaner took off. Fred Smith almost went broke getting FedEx off the ground. If you have an idea that could change the world, be responsible. Don't put your family's basic needs at risk. Make sure that your idea is good enough that you can spread your risk by getting investors on board.

**Market to a niche.** If you can't change the world, dominate a niche. Choose a specific target market that you know or like, and come up with ideas to serve the people in that market. For instance, create products and services for businesses in a specific industry. Serve the needs of people with specific hobbies and interests, like golf, motorcycles, heavy metal music, or photography. Focus on serving people with similar beliefs, like fundamental Christians or liberal Democrats. Build a business around people who went to the same or similar schools, the way that one entrepreneur built a dating service specifically for Ivy League graduates.

**Build a company that is faster, better, and/or cheaper.** Entrepreneur Nick Veneris, CEO of Xomba.com, advises, "Concern yourself more with improving an already existing idea rather than stressing over inventing the wheel. Lots of companies have great ideas, but execute poorly. Capitalize on this." What can you do faster than other companies? How might you provide better service, quality, or results? How can you offer lower prices? These are common questions to answer in order to come up with a new business. FedEx is generally faster and more reliable than the United States Postal Service, but the United States Postal Service is cheaper. Wal-Mart and Southwest

Air are famous for creating business systems that allow them to offer lower prices. Papa John's Pizza competed against Domino's by claiming to use better ingredients to create better pizza.

**Read entrepreneurial publications and websites.** Every aspiring entrepreneur should subscribe to *Entrepreneur Magazine* and other entrepreneurial publications. You should also go online and become active on every website you can that focuses on entrepreneurs.

**Use search engines.** When I first started out as an entrepreneur, there was no Google. If I were starting out today, I'd spend hours using search engines to look for new business opportunities. Search for industry trends, demographic trends, hot new start-ups, new franchises, fastest growing businesses, initial public offerings, venture capital investments, angel investors, entrepreneur awards, entrepreneurs to watch, lists of entrepreneurs, and lists of promising businesses.

**Get involved in business associations.** Follow the membership of companies like the Young Presidents' Organization, Vistage International, and others that bring together CEOs of growing companies. Get active in your local Chamber of Commerce and take a leadership role in their entrepreneurial and economic development initiatives. Join associations in your industry and meet people who are starting new ventures, while keeping an eye out for interesting trends and opportunities.

**Piggyback on others starting or investing in businesses.** Instead of coming up with your own good idea, connect with people who have their own good ideas and are starting businesses. If you have skills to offer them, you can join their start-up team with an ownership share.

**Help experts expand their reach.** Many experts would like to become better known in their markets, and you can help. In my case, I've found a number of fitness experts who are brilliant at what they do and partnered with them to offer fitness certification programs to the public. My site www. fitnessnichecompany.com offers fitness certifications in agility, unique strength and conditioning programs, boxing fitness, kickboxing fitness, and self-defense. You can work with experts to develop intellectual capital and then market it to the public for a share of the revenues you generate. Alternatively, you can help experts get endorsement deals or get booked as speakers and take a cut of the opportunities you create. You can also become a broker of experts by starting up a focused recruiting or staffing firm.

**License other people's intellectual property.** There is a lot of great content out there. Authors, business owners, inventors, professors, and universities often own valuable ideas and technology that they can't market successfully. You can help. For instance, a colleague of mine—with no previous experience in chemistry—licensed the rights to market a university technology that could extract gold from mining sludge, helping mining companies extract even more value from their mining properties. This entrepreneur also hired the professor who developed the invention as his chief scientific officer; together, they are working on raising funds and developing the technology into a full-fledged business.

Another colleague of mine licenses self-help content from publishing houses and develops subscription-based websites based on that content. His websites help people lose weight, get more organized, manage their time, and have happier marriages. His customers pay him a monthly subscription in exchange for a system that gets results for them.

In my own case, I have found ambitious entrepreneurs in Asia, the United Kingdom, and Mexico who have licensed my executive coach training materials and are marketing them to those overseas markets. They are providing translation, local marketing, and programs that fit specific cultures—all in exchange for a fair share of the revenues they generate.

**Learn from franchises.** Every day new franchises start up and recruit people to buy a territory and expand their brand. While you might consider buying a franchise, you can also study these businesses and identify opportunities. Many of these businesses are still new enough that they have little but a logo, an operating manual, and a few locations. At the same time, a common complaint of many franchisees is, "I can't believe I paid all of this money for nothing. I could have started this business on my own, and now I'm stuck paying royalties to the folks at headquarters, and they don't do much for me in return." You can avoid their mistakes by identifying strong concepts and building competing businesses—with no territory restrictions—on your own.

**Meet with business brokers in your area.** Business brokers can provide you with listings of businesses for sale. You can either buy a business from them or get ideas from the would-be sellers to start your own competing business.

**Get ideas from the *Yellow Pages*.** Again, a business doesn't have to be earth-shattering, or even new, to be successful—especially if you are willing to hustle for customers and go out of your way to delight them. The traditional *Yellow Pages* book may be a declining product, but it is filled with page after page of business ideas. Go through your local *Yellow Pages*. Study the different ways that businesses advertise and compete. Look for categories of businesses with fewer listings than you would expect, and categories that seem to project a less professional image than you would have thought. Find categories that seem interesting to you. If you had to choose one business to start based on what you read in this directory, what would it be? If you are really courageous, close your eyes and open a page at random. Come up with a plan to start your own business in that category, simply as a thought exercise. Who knows? It could lead to something.

**Meet with local commercial bankers and SBA lenders.** Ask a local commercial banker out for coffee. Tell the banker that you are interested in starting a business and wonder if he would mind if you picked his brain. In addition to asking about the bank's requirements for lending money, ask about the bank's recent commercial and SBA loan activity and for his perspective on business opportunities in town.

**Learn from companies growing at business incubators.** Business incubators offer space and support for new businesses. Go to the National Business Incubator Association website at www.nbia.org and study various incubators nationwide. Check out the kinds of businesses that different incubators are supporting. You might get some great ideas based on those that other creative business owners are pursuing.

**Learn from other growing companies.** Study the *Inc. 500* and *Business Week* lists of fastest growing companies, the *Business 2.0* list of fastest growing technology companies, and other lists of growing companies.

**Come up with new service delivery models.** Think about a new way to deliver services. For instance, law firms are sprouting up that don't follow the tired old billable-hours model. Instead, they place attorneys into companies as interim corporate counsel or part of the legal team—at a salary. That way, companies get top legal talent at down-to-earth rates. They don't have to worry about paying $500 per hour for a simple phone call.

**Bring overseas trends here.** Business opportunities that start overseas could be poised to explode here. They only need someone like you to find them and bring them over. Karaoke, anime, and robot dogs started out in Asia and have become big in the United States. Pick a country that you love and spend some time there, looking for new products that you might be able to bring back with you or adapt. A friend of mine who worked for a multi-national agricultural company and was based in Ecuador started buying up art from South American artists while he traveled the continent. He sells this art to United States collectors at a nice profit.

Similarly, when Mike Symczak and his business partner Jason Lucash were traveling in South Korea, they saw a box-shaped, hard plastic speaker for sale. They immediately thought to themselves, "We would do well if we could make something like this out of recycled materials, and have it be collapsible, like a Chinese food takeout box." While in Korea, they contacted manufacturers and commissioned a prototype. Their company, OrigAudio was born, and shortly afterwards, *Time Magazine* named their invention one of the top 50 inventions of the year.

Of course, the same concept works in reverse. You can bring trends from your country to other markets, too—if you have or can make the connections.

**Explore outsourcing trends.** Instead of complaining or worrying that your job will be outsourced, take advantage of the trend. For instance, a colleague of mine has built a multi-million dollar business finding the best software experts from around the world; he markets this talent to companies looking for leading-edge software solutions without having to pay $150 per hour for US-based software developers. A friend of mine who is of Indian descent created an Indian-based call center with his cousins, who are all based in Mumbai. Almost any kind of professional in the United States—including attorneys, accountants, salespeople, and engineers—have counterparts in emerging markets who are trained equally well but work for much less. You can resist this trend and face the consequences, or you can embrace it and build a business around it.

**Plan to be bought out by a larger company.** If you had to develop a company so that Microsoft, Google, Nike, or another large corporation wanted to buy you out, what kind of company would you start? The ultimate dream of many entrepreneurs is that a much bigger company will take notice of their venture and buy it. Pick a large company in your area or on the *Fortune 500* list and study it. Where are they heading? What kind of unique expertise might they be interested in acquiring? Many big companies don't have the speed, flexibility, or creativity to come up with leading-edge ideas on their own. They have to grow by buying companies that do. You can start one, first by thinking about the kinds of innovation, new products, and growth these companies need.

**Do some fringe reading.** Fringe publications on the web and at newsstands can help you uncover new ideas. Make it a habit every week to read at least one publication that is way outside your comfort zone. Read about pro wrestling, extreme science, politics, global trends, fitness, health, spiritual pursuits, and adventure.

**Exploit the government.** The United States government puts out tons of information every year that can't be copyrighted. Take that information, make it easy for people to digest and read, and sell it. That's what Matthew Lesko has done. Perhaps you have seen him in his unique green question mark suit pitching his products. Matthew researches government grant and loan opportunities, packages this information, and sells it on infomercials. There's no magic to what he does, except for having a talent for creative marketing. There are many other opportunities to repackage government information: analyzing bills that Congress passes, providing easy-to-read advice about navigating government departments, and letting frustrated taxpayers know about pork-barrel and inefficient spending.

**Hold brainstorming sessions with friends and colleagues.** Multiple minds are usually better than one. Have a monthly or weekly meeting with friends, specifically designed to come up with new business ideas. Set a goal to come up with ten good ideas before the meeting ends. Have someone write down the ideas. Agree to the brainstorming ground rule that no idea is a bad idea. Get as many ideas as you can down on paper, and then flesh out a few of the more exciting ones.

**Get the rights to ideas that your employer rejects.** If your employer rejects an idea that you like, get permission to build a company around the idea. A business school classmate of mine came up with the idea for an online auction site to help big businesses get supplies at lower costs. He brought the idea to executives at his company, and they rejected it. He launched the idea on his own and ended up selling out for tens of millions of dollars.

**Outsource your job.** Your current employer could be your first client. If you work at a company that is looking to reduce costs, and you think that your job might be at risk, consider approaching your employer and suggesting that they outsource your job or department…to you. The first chapter introduced you to Patricia Kilgore, who proposed to her CEO that she run her marketing department on an outsourced basis. The CEO accepted, and her marketing and public relations firm was born.

**Buy all or part of your current employer's business.** Why leave your job if your best entrepreneurial opportunity is right where you work? You might be able to own all or part of your current employer. The gentleman who cleans our pool used to be an employee at the pool services company he now owns. Then he made an offer to buy the company from his boss. Now he is growing the business on his own terms. He is training other employees to take over the routes and is starting to grow the business while others do the work.

Be careful with this strategy. Sometimes the owner of a business will make vague promises to you in order to keep you working for him. For instance, the owner of a retail store has been promising a nephew of mine that he will turn over his business to him someday. However, the owner hasn't put anything in writing, hasn't set specific milestones for the transfer, and hasn't discussed terms. I wish that my nephew were more assertive and willing to pin down this owner on exactly how the ownership transfer will happen. Until he does, he is living in a dream world and can't count on ever owning this business.

**Work for a company that accelerates your career and gets you into the deal flow.** There are three types of companies where, as an employee, you get access to opportunities, deals, and experiences that other companies can't provide. First, many MBAs go to work for consulting firms because they get to work with top decision makers and tend to be on the leading edge of new business ideas and trends. Second, people who work at commercial banks, venture capital firms, hedge funds, and private equity firms get access to people with capital and learn how to find and make lucrative deals. Third, mid-sized, rapidly growing firms tend to give you lots of opportunities to grow and be creative, without having the capital issues that tiny companies face or the huge bureaucracies that hinder employees at larger companies. Many entrepreneurs launch businesses after working at these three types of companies, because they get terrific exposure, experience, industry insights, and contacts.

**Connect to serial entrepreneurs who need help.** Some people have more good ideas than they know what to do with. They often seek out smart, energetic people—like you—to run businesses for them in exchange for sweat equity. Look for these people in your community. You will read about them in the paper, meet them at the Chamber of Commerce, and see them hanging out with other entrepreneurs. A colleague of mine grew three businesses for one of these serial entrepreneurs after he graduated from college. He made enough money from this work to travel the world and then pay his way through business school.

Did you come up with at least five ideas, or ways to tap into ideas, from the above sources? If not, go through the list again until you do. What is your next step for you to flesh out each idea?

In my own case, coming up with ideas has always been the easy part. I can remember dreaming up all sorts of good and bad product and business ideas since I was 16 years old. For me, the challenge has been taking ideas, tossing the bad ones without wasting time or money on them, fleshing out the good ones, taking smart action, getting those first customers, and growing healthy businesses from there. A good idea is only a starting point. In other words, you still have many battles left to win. The book turns to your next battle now....

## Chapter Three

# BATTLE NUMBER THREE:

## Get Strong Support from Family, Friends, and Your Network of Colleagues

T he third battle you must win in order to start a business and escape your job is to get support from other people. There are two fronts to this battle. The first front is to surround yourself with positive people who support your goals. This is the easier of the two fronts, because there are many, many people and resources who are delighted help you. You simply need to take action to surround yourself with them.

The second, more challenging, front is dealing with the people—perhaps including the people closest to you—who intentionally or unintentionally are not on board with what you are trying to achieve. When you start a new business, you become somebody different than the person you used to be. You are more independent, courageous, creative, and adventurous. Meanwhile, your friends and family have a pre-existing image of you. Some of them might feel threatened, afraid, jealous, or cynical about what you are trying to achieve and what it might mean for their own security.

Let's start with your significant other, if you have one. Your spouse has a huge impact on how easy or hard your start-up experience is going to be. A classic movie example of this is from *Rocky III*. In this installment of the series, Rocky loses his urge to fight. His trainer can't motivate him to get his edge back, and Rocky can't seem to get motivated on his own. Finally, his wife Adrian sets him straight. Her pep talk helps him get back his confidence and intensity. Whether you like the *Rocky* films or not, Rocky's relationship with his wife shows how important a spouse can be to anyone trying to achieve greatness.

There are many issues that you have to discuss with your spouse in order to avoid distracting conflicts once you start taking action on your business. John Fortin, founder of www.grandmonadnockstore.com, tells his story in a way that makes the potential tension between spouses almost palpable: "When I started tossing around the idea of starting an online store, my wife was absolutely livid!!! She told me, 'This is a waste of time and money, it will never work, etc., etc., etc.!' I told her I would spend MY MONEY so if it did not work out she would not be able to hold the monetary loss over my head. I also got her involved in the building of the store, so she would not complain about my spending more time on the store than with her."

Similarly, Mark A. Piatt, of Optimum Service Solutions, shares the following experience about a business he started while also juggling a full-time job and going back to school for an advanced degree: "There were many times when my wife and I would argue about which was more important, spending quality time with the family or bringing home the bacon so that we could enjoy the family vacations that we had grown accustomed to taking."

In my own case, both my wife and I have started a few businesses, and we've become acutely aware of the conflicts that can arise when one spouse starts something new. Based on this experience and what other entrepreneurs have shared with me, following are five issues that you have to resolve with your significant other and immediate family before you make the leap:

- **One: Make sure the foundation of your relationship is solid.** A strong relationship is based on unconditional love—in both sickness and health, and whether you are rich or poor. Meanwhile, a new business can put big strains on any relationship, no matter how strong. That's because you are asking your partner to share in the uncertainty that comes with any business venture, but without giving them much, if any, control. Even if the relationship is strong, you can expect conflicts to break out. If the relationship is weak, these conflicts can seriously strain the relationship and potentially tear it apart. For instance, a few years ago I started up a foolhardy business venture that lost tons of money before I hit my stop loss and decided to shut it down. If I had kept going, I would have caused my family financial hardship. At some point in this scary process, I had a heart-to-heart conversation with my wife about the fact that the business wasn't going to make it. I felt quite insecure about my business acumen at that point, and about my future financial prospects in general. I was so doubtful that I even asked my wife if she would love me even if we had to live in a trailer. She knew about the business and understood what I was asking. Bless her heart, because she told me she loved me and would stay with me no matter what. She added, "But let's close this business down now, okay?" I sincerely hope that you can have that kind of open conversation with your spouse—during the good, the bad, and the uncertain times of your business start-up.

- **Two: Agree on the family's budget.** Mike Scanlin, CEO of BornToSell.com, which offers covered call investment tools, writes, "Explain that there will be small, inexpensive vacations for the next couple of years, if at all. Get their buy-in or the cost of building your business will be your relationship." Starting a business can have a significant impact on the family's finances and budget. Work together with your spouse to lay out a plan, and get everyone on board.

- **Three: Agree on how much you will be available for the family.** A business is a demanding mistress. It will compete for your attention with your family. The way you spend your time will change, and probably not for the better from their vantage point. Make sure your family understands this reality and can handle it.

- **Four: Set ground rules about giving and getting advice and on the spouse's role.** I will never forget the sound the stapler made when it whizzed by my head and hit the wall...after I gave my wife some unsolicited advice about how she was running one of her businesses. Like it or not, your spouse will want to be involved in this exciting new venture. While you might not be open to their business coaching, it might be smart on your part to prepare yourself for it, because that's what you are probably going to get. Be open to hearing your spouse's advice. Don't get defensive about it, and don't insult their ideas. Instead, thank them for any constructive advice that they might give you, and consider whether you can use it. At the same time, if the spouse wants to be involved in the business as more than a Monday-morning quarterback, then he or she needs clear accountability. You don't want someone coming in and out of the business at will, offering opinions and helping here and there, but without being on the hook for results. Separate the romantic relationship from the business relationship, hard as that may be to do. Create a job description, including key performance indicators and how the reporting relationship works.

- **Five: Agree on exact milestones for what success means and when it is time to quit.** You need to avoid putting your family at risk by exhausting more of your funds than your spouse is comfortable spending, and your spouse needs to support you as long as the business is meeting agreed-upon goals. Therefore, create a contract with your spouse based on key milestones that the business needs to achieve. If the business is meeting those milestones, your spouse agrees to support you. He or she can't arbitrarily say, "We need more money. Close the business down now and go back to your old job." At the same time, if the business isn't meeting the agreed-upon milestones, you should shut down the business and do something else. For instance, agree on a date when you need to get your first customer, when you need to replace half of your previous salary, and when you need to be making as much as you were as an employee.

Your spouse is only one member of your family. As soon as you let people know that you are starting a business, other members of your family will feel free to chime in with their ideas and try to get involved. Some of them will have good intentions, while others might not. Regardless, unless you have a family member who has a track record of success and has done something similar to what you are trying to do, consider the possibility that their advice—no matter how helpful they are trying to be—will be worthless, if not counterproductive. Anand Bhatt, founder and CEO of record label Sonic Wave International, advises, "Do the opposite of what your friends and family advise. Unless they are absolutely successful in the niche you are getting into, ignore them." Similarly, you read earlier about George Zaharoff and how members of his family kept telling him to get out of the business, and—when he hit setbacks—let him know in no uncertain terms that they knew he would never succeed. Give some thought ahead of time to which members of your family will provide unwanted advice, as well as who will act like snipers and try to shoot down your confidence, especially when you feel most vulnerable. How will you handle them when they do?

Some family members might be willing, and even offer, to invest in your idea. This is a tempting situation, but before you accept, think hard about whether you want to mix family with business. Do you really want your father-in-law looking over your shoulder and questioning every decision you make? At the same time, if you take family money and your business doesn't work out, you might damage the relationship for life. As one entrepreneur, who wishes to remain anonymous, shared, "I received a $22,000 investment from my cousin, and the business failed. He wanted me to pay him back but, per our written agreement, he was buying a share of the business, not providing a loan. We haven't spoken for five years." Instead of taking money from family, try to bootstrap your idea on your own. If you need investors, seek money from people with whom you have an arms' length relationship. That way, you get objective outsiders to take a hard look at your business and you don't complicate your business any more than necessary.

Once your immediate family is on board and you are ready to deal with what other family members might say or do, your next step is to develop a support network that extends beyond your family. This is your group of trusted friends, colleagues, and mentors to whom you can turn when you need help, advice, or support.

There is a balance to strike when you reach out to your network. On the one hand, you don't want to hold back and miss out on getting immediate support from your colleagues. To repeat what entrepreneur Sharron Jones shared in a previous chapter, "I could have used my network to build my client list far faster and become more profitable sooner if I hadn't been afraid that my existing contacts would snicker up their sleeves at my business idea."

At the same time, you don't want your contacts to think you are a flake. I have a friend who frequently starts businesses that sputter out, and she tells her entire network about them before she should. For instance, she recently started a blog that she was sure, as she wrote in an email, was her "passion in life." She sent out emails to all of her friends and family asking them to look at her blog and give her advice. She got her parents to do the same thing to their network. Within two weeks, she lost interest and shut the whole project down. How likely do you think her network and family will be to go out on a limb for her the next time she has an impulse to start a business?

When you create your support network, be politically smart about it. Start with your inner circle of most trusted friends and colleagues, people who stick with you through thick and thin and forgive you when you stumble. Then, as you get surer about your direction, involve the next layer of colleagues. Keep expanding from there.

In the table below, list up to 10 people you know who can provide some form of tangible or intangible support as you get your business going. Write some notes about what they can bring to you, such as emotional support, mentoring, great ideas, contacts, functional or technical skills, leads, and funding. Also, write down when you should get them involved in your venture. For instance, if you know some heavy hitters, people with real influence and resources, but you don't know them well, you might get only one shot to ask them for help; it might make sense to wait until your business gets some traction.

## TOP TEN PEOPLE WHO WILL PROVIDE SUPPORT FOR YOUR BUSINESS

| Name | How They Can Provide Support | Point At Which You Will Contact Them |
|------|------------------------------|--------------------------------------|
|      |                              |                                      |
|      |                              |                                      |
|      |                              |                                      |
|      |                              |                                      |
|      |                              |                                      |
|      |                              |                                      |
|      |                              |                                      |
|      |                              |                                      |
|      |                              |                                      |
|      |                              |                                      |

As you review the above list, what conclusions can you draw about your support network? If you need to strengthen it, who are five people on the above list who can introduce you to additional people?

Meanwhile, think about the best way you can educate people about your new business. Be sure you can tell them exactly what kind of support you want from them. If you want leads, be prepared to describe exactly the type of person or business that would be an ideal lead for you. Also, be ready to ask about specific people they might know who might be interested in your business. For instance, if they are on the board of a prominent non-profit, ask them who else on the board might have a need for your services or products.

---

## THE IMPORTANCE OF HAVING A MENTOR

One common theme among the entrepreneurs in this book was the importance of having a mentor, or a group of mentors. For instance, Kristy Dunn Fox, owner of KD Fox and Associates, writes, "My carefully selected mentor/coach is a successful, experienced peer in my industry who has personally attained the kind of commercial and financial success I aspire to. She keeps the complicated information from my other sources boiled down to a practical level so I can move forward without falling into the trap of analysis paralysis." If you are lucky enough to find a single person willing to assume the role of mentor, such as a former boss or a seasoned entrepreneur who decides to take you under his or her wing, congratulations. If not, you can assemble everything you would want in a single mentor by learning bits and pieces from various successful people in your network. The ways that people have found mentors include: nurturing relationships with former colleagues and bosses; joining social or athletic clubs, where you can meet successful people in a more relaxed context; joining the board of a local non-profit, where other board members see your skills firsthand; joining—or starting—a networking group specific to your profile, for instance, a networking group for mompreneurs; taking a leadership role at your industry or functional association; and reaching out to successful people in your industry, so that you can ask them for their advice.

---

In addition, think about people that you don't know now but that you would like to know, because they can help you as you grow your business. Who are potential mentors? Who might be able to give you valuable advice or open doors for you? Who are people who are doing great things in your target market? Don't let your own beliefs about yourself limit your willingness to get out there and tell others about your business. Many successful people love giving advice to up-and-coming entrepreneurs. You just have to be open to advice and take action to reach out to them. A number of very successful people have agreed to meet me for coffee or an informational interview at their office, only because I emailed them, reached out to them on LinkedIn, or picked up the phone and called. In other cases, I didn't know the person myself but found someone who did. The worst that can happen is they don't respond or say no. Big deal! If they decline, reach out to someone else.

In the table below, list five people you don't know now but would like to know because they can help you with your business.

| WISH LIST: PEOPLE TO GET TO KNOW AND ENLIST FOR SUPPORT | | |
|---|---|---|
| Name | Date By Which I Will Reach Out | How I Will Reach Out |
| | | |
| | | |
| | | |
| | | |
| | | |

Now you have lists of people who you know and need to know who can help you in your business. There are many other ways for you to get support while you test and grow your business. Based on a survey put out to thousands of entrepreneurs, following is a list of the most commonly mentioned people, groups, places, resources, and activities that entrepreneurs rely on for support—in addition to their regular network of friends and colleagues:

1. Make an appointment with SCORE, the Service Corps of Retired Executives. Get free business consulting and an objective review of your business idea.

2. Check into Small Business Development Centers, or SBDCs. See www.sba.com for a list of SBDCs that might be able to assist your business and provide support.

3. Join industry and professional associations and trade groups. Be sure to get active in a leadership role. That way, you meet the heavy hitters and they see that you are somebody who can make things happen.

4. Consult your professional advisors, including your attorney, accountant, web designer, information technology expert, and insurance broker. While these professionals get paid for their services, the best ones usually won't charge for answering quick questions or providing an occasional consultation—especially to a solid long-term client.

5. Connect with known experts and opinion leaders in your industry. Read what they have to say and reach out and contact them for advice.

6. Meet with vendors who supply goods and services to your target market or in your industry. They will want to help you because you might become a customer.

7. Sign up for free teleseminars from industry gurus and consultants.

8. Create an advisory board. Invite professionals you respect to join. Their role is to be there for you as a sounding board for new ideas. They can also add credibility to your business.

9. Create or join a business club. Invite other entrepreneurs to meet monthly to support one another and share ideas.

10. Create a mastermind group of a few like-minded professionals who meet to solve problems, support each other, and even exchange leads. Howard Sherman, owner of RoyalGeeks.com, writes, "On occasion I'll set up a mastermind group as put forth in Napoleon Hill's *Think and Grow Rich,* where a number of us entrepreneurs sit down together and work out a common problem, the solution to which benefits us all."

11. Join local networking groups, including specialty groups for your gender, age group, industry, life stage, religion, or ethnicity. For instance, Nedra Rezinas, owner of blue deer designs llc, says, "This has been one of the best ways to connect with other like-minded business owners. I'm becoming a mom in December, so I've recently joined a local Portland Mother Business Owners group. It's been a great place to find support as my life and business changes with a child in the mix!" By the way, if you can't find a group that fits you, start one.

12. Do periodic retreats with one or more colleagues to plan out your business goals for the coming quarter or year.

13. Get involved in the community and give something back, while meeting other community leaders.

14. Join the local Chamber of Commerce. If you run a business that targets local customers, Chamber membership can be a good investment. As with any association membership, don't expect to get benefits if you don't participate. Get active as a leader, for instance, as an ambassador or a volunteer on a committee.

15. Your local college or university might have a small business outreach program.

16. Go online and join a service like www.solorevolution.com.

17. Use the local library. A number of entrepreneurs report that they go there to take advantage of the library's many free resources and sources of information.

18. Read industry trade journals and visit websites dedicated to your industry.

19. Participate in online groups at LinkedIn and Facebook, as well as in groups formed at the websites of various small business publications, like *Inc., Entrepreneur*, and the American Express Open Forum.

20. Join groups of local entrepreneurs who meet via www.meetup.com. However, avoid groups that are run by people making a blatant sales pitch for their consulting or coaching services.

21. Ask questions and provide answers on Q&A sites like www.answers.com.

22. Use Twitter. Nedra Rezinas, quoted earlier in this section, says, "I've connected with people locally on Twitter and gone to tweetups, where I meet people in person and get a chance to really talk to them. It's also been great to ask questions on Twitter, get real answers, and meet folks as it happens."

23. Take an improvisational or stand-up comedy class. Life Coach Donna Stellhorn suggested this idea, which she did to, as she says, "add some flair" to her public speaking. It also seems like a great way to meet other people, get better at improvising, and gain confidence.

24. Take up a hobby or a sport and use it as a way to recharge.

25. Budget specific times to be with family and, during these times, turn off your mobile devices and put them away.

26. Learn to meditate or do yoga to relax and get grounded.

27. Build in breaks during the day to relax, exercise, and recharge.

In the table below, write down five ideas that you will use from the above list, or from your own ideas, so that you have additional support as you get your business going.

| FIVE OTHER IDEAS TO GET SUPPORT WHILE GROWING THE BUSINESS | |
| --- | --- |
| Idea to Get Support, Including How Often You Will Participate: | Starting When? |
| | |
| | |
| | |
| | |
| | |

There is one more thing you need to do to make sure you get the support you need for your business: Shed people from your network who are going to be cynical or even try to thwart what you are doing. Starting a business puts you in a vulnerable place. You can't afford to hang out with people who are negative or who don't have your best interests in mind. Of course, it can be very valuable to have devil's advocates in your network, people who have your best interests at heart and challenge your ideas with solid logic. However, you don't want to have naysayers who are being negative because they feel jealous, are threatened by your initiative, or don't want to see you succeed while they stay stuck where they are.

List anyone you think you might need to avoid, or even shed from your network, so that you surround yourself with positive people.

## NEGATIVE PEOPLE TO SHED FROM YOUR NETWORK:

## SHOULD YOU HAVE A PARTNER?
### One Entrepreneur Shares Her Experience.

Some people do better with a business partner, and some do worse. My wife and I have had bad experiences with our respective business partners: conflicting styles, different aspirations, differing abilities to contribute money, different time lines, and different work ethics. We have learned that we need to fly solo, and aren't good with business partners. Following is a story and advice from Carol Galle, CMP of Special D Events, Inc., who has found that a partner provides her with a crucial source of support:

My greatest fear was going it alone. I realized early on that business owners have a tremendous weight on their shoulders and, frankly, I didn't want to be the only one lying in bed at night unable to sleep because of that burden. In addition, I knew that owning a business could be very isolating. I wanted to be able to bounce ideas off someone else on a daily basis, and employees and family are not always an option. So for me, a partner was the best solution.

Partnerships are not for everyone, but my suggestions for a successful relationship are as follows:

1. If possible, choose someone who has as much to lose and gain as you do. The level of risk should be similar for both parties.

2. Avoid choosing a friend or relative. It's much easier to tackle the tough issues with someone with whom you have always had a business relationship.

*continued on next page…*

*...continued from previous page*

3. Choose a good attorney and draft all the appropriate documents up front, including the partnership agreement, buy/sell agreement, and succession plan. Obviously, as time goes on you will want to update some of those documents, but it's important to have an existing base.

4. Expect that you will live and breathe with this person for a long time to come. Petty annoyances can become major grievances in such close quarters. Be prepared to give and take. It's essentially a marriage!

## Chapter Four

# BATTLE NUMBER FOUR:
## Develop a Strategy That Gives You an Edge

I f you have a dream to start a business and you look in the phone book or do an online search of the number of companies in your industry, you might become overwhelmed. Your research might uncover hundreds or even thousands of competitors in your local area alone. How in the world do you become visible and stand out with all of this competition?

The answer is: develop a winning strategy. That way, you stand out and gain an edge over your competition, even in what might seem like a crowded marketplace. This chapter shows you how to do that, using a simple, powerful, and buzzword-free step-by-step process.

I wish I had a process like this to follow when I started my business. My strategy course at Harvard Business School, based on the work of a well-known strategy guru, was almost unintelligible to me. All of the case studies in that course focused on massive, extremely complex companies and the well-paid executives leading them. I couldn't relate. After business school, I kept reading books and articles about strategy in the hopes of finding an easy-to-understand system. Unfortunately, many of the books, journals, and seminars about strategy were packed with jargon that made the expert seem really smart but ended up being more confusing than helpful. When you start a new business, do you really need to understand buzzwords like: sustainable competitive advantage, best of breed, co-opetition, competitive ecosystem, repurpose, synergize, dis-intermediate, core competencies, systems archetypes, stakeholders, burning platform, leveling the playing field, actionable, incentivize, randomized Monte Carlo scenarios, or learning organization? No, you don't.

What you do need is to figure out how your business is going to stand apart so that people want to spend money with you, especially when they have many other options, including the option of doing nothing at all. To demonstrate how strategy works, let's start with an example from an industry that everyone knows a little bit about. In my hometown there are many, many real estate brokers. There is even a joke that when police officers pull you over here, they ask for your real estate license instead of your driver's license. While the market here might seem saturated after a casual look in the phone book, savvy real estate brokers have found many different ways to compete and gain an edge. Here are only a few of the ways that the best of them succeed:

- **Geography.** Many real estate brokers specialize in serving a single subdivision. That way, residents in that subdivision perceive them to be the expert in their neighborhood. Brokers who use this strategy get active in the subdivision, send out market research reports to residents, and hold educational seminars for residents about real estate trends in the area.

- **Luxury.** Some brokers focus only on the top end of the market: mansions, waterfront properties, and high-end condos. They develop relationships with the luxury builders and developers in town and set up exclusive deals to market their properties. They also know how to network with the wealthy residents in the community by joining the right country clubs and being part of the right social circles.

- **Waterfront.** A few brokers only handle properties on the ocean, bay, or lakes. Those types of properties are in big demand here, and some buyers only want waterfront.

- **Golf course.** Similarly, many people move to my area to live in a golf course community, and some brokers specialize in that niche.

- **Vacation investments and rentals.** Some investors buy and sell vacation rentals. Specialized brokers respond by focusing on the needs of these buyers, including services that attract snowbirds and vacationers from the north.

- **Foreclosures and short sales.** During the housing bust of 2008, many brokers became experts at helping people buy and sell distressed properties.

- **Buyers only.** At least one real estate broker in town heavily advertises that he only serves buyers. In exchange for a commission, he helps buyers find their ideal property and negotiate against brokers who represent the seller.

- **One-stop shopping.** Some of the larger firms compete partly based on their ability to handle everything involved in a sale: staging the property, mortgages, title, closing, and specialized legal services.

- **Experience.** One firm claims that its brokers have more experience than other firms. They have systems in place to attract seasoned brokers who don't want to run their own business but who do want special incentives based on their track record and experience in the market.

- **Multi-family properties.** A few brokers are known for their expertise in helping people buy, sell, and rent multi-family properties.

- **Commercial.** One firm in town is famous for having bright red and yellow signs in front of commercial properties for sale or for lease. People think of this company first when they want to buy, sell, or lease commercial property.

- **International.** Because the dollar is low compared to currencies in many other countries, some brokers organize tours of international visitors seeking to buy first or second homes here. They even have a fancy tour bus that escorts visitors around town to view select properties.

- **Discount listings.** Many brokers list properties for half the going rate. In exchange, they provide a-la-carte, no-frills services.

- **Technology.** Some brokers have invested heavily in technology that markets their listed properties all over the Internet, with an emphasis on getting their listings ranked at the top of search engines.

- **Alliances and networking.** A large number of brokers here succeed because they are outstanding networkers. They get active on non-profit boards, join clubs, and participate in the community. That way, people know them and call them first when it is time to buy or sell their homes.

The purpose of the above list is to demonstrate, based on a single industry as an example, how business owners find different ways to compete and gain an edge. This is especially the case in crowded markets, where it is easy to jump in and start a business. When the housing bust hit in 2008, almost every real estate professional in my town suffered a devastating blow. The ones who survived did so because they had either carved out a solid niche or they quickly shifted to the new growth niche of foreclosures and short sales. Those who dabbled in the field as a hobby, or who didn't have a way to stand out from the crowd, quit. They had no trouble finding business when the market was booming, but when they bubble burst, they were doomed.

The above list shows that regardless of the type of business you intend to start, you need to figure out how your business is going to compete. You can't be successful by offering the same products and services as everyone else. You need a strategy that defines how your business will position itself in the market and how it will gain a significant edge that matters to buyers. Following is a five-step process for you to develop your competitive strategy, so that you have an edge and your business is poised to win.

---

## FIVE-STEP STRATEGIC PLANNING PROCESS FOR A NEW BUSINESS

1. What problem do you solve, and for whom?
2. Who are your competitors?
3. What is your edge?
4. How can you reduce the risk that buyers might feel before doing business with you?
5. What will be your marketing message to compel people to take interest?

---

Let's explore each step...

## ONE: WHAT PROBLEM DO YOU SOLVE, AND FOR WHOM?

Some businesses make the huge mistake of building their strategy based on what they want to do, and not what the market wants to buy. They come up with an interesting idea and try to figure out how to get other people to see value in it. That's backwards. The dot-com era at the turn of this century was littered with failed companies that were launched this way. These entrepreneurs came up with a nifty website or technology and tried to push their concept into the market, as in: "Here is our solution. Now, what's your problem?"

The more effective approach is to start with a pressing problem that causes pain for lots of people and then solve it. That way, you start with other people's needs first, and then come up with something that they will find valuable. If you start here, you have a much better chance of offering a service or product that the people in your target market won't be able to resist, once they hear about it.

So, what problem do you solve, and for whom? Let's break this question down into two parts, starting with the second part: Who is your ideal customer?

Many businesses incorrectly think that everyone is a customer. That assumption can be costly. While it may give you false hope to think that the size of your target market is unlimited, it is much better to choose a focused target market. With a focused target market, you may have fewer potential buyers, but you end up making bigger profits. That's because with a clearly defined target market:

- You reach buyers more easily and less expensively. People in the same target market tend to read similar publications, go to similar websites, join the same groups, and attend the same events.

- You don't waste money trying to court people who aren't going to be your customers.

- You convert more prospects to buyers. That's because people in a specific target market appreciate it when you understand their unique problems, talk their language, and create products and services especially for them.

- You get people talking about you, because people in the same target market tend to know each other and share information about great new products and services.

- You beat out generalists who continue to believe that everyone is a potential customer.

As the case of the real estate industry showed, there are many types of target markets. You can even combine some of the different possibilities listed below and come up with a super-focused target market:

- **Industry,** like healthcare, financial services, or semiconductors.
- **Job function,** like CEO or Human Resources Manager.
- **Geographic location,** such as a country, region, state, city, zip code, area code, or neighborhood.
- **Demographic profile,** including age, generation, gender, income, education, religion, and ethnicity.
- **Psychographic profile,** including hobbies, values, political affiliation, and strong beliefs about certain issues. For instance, many companies now target consumers who care a lot about the environment and are willing to spend more money to support eco-friendly products. You can target stay-at-home moms, fundamentalist Christians, motorcycle enthusiasts, video game addicts, far-left liberals, and Tea Party supporters—and that's only the beginning of the possibilities.

Once you identify your target market, your next mission is to identify a big problem that the people in that market face, one that you can solve. If you can complete any of the following sentences, you have probably identified a serious problem that people in your target market will pay money to solve:

## WORKSHEET: IDENTIFYING A PAINFUL PROBLEM TO SOLVE

| Start with one of these phrases: | Describe a problem that completes the sentence: | Example |
|---|---|---|
| Stop struggling with…. | | Stop struggling to build your medical practice. |
| Stop worrying about…. | | Stop worrying about whether your kids will get into a good college. |
| Stop wasting your time on…. | | Stop wasting your time paying and mailing bills. |

| | | |
|---|---|---|
| Continued from previous page. | | |
| **Start with one of these phrases:** | **Describe a problem that completes the sentence:** | **Example** |
| Stop wasting money on.... | | Stop wasting money on your phone bill. |
| Stop paying too much for.... | | Stop paying too much for car insurance. |
| Stop tolerating.... | | Stop tolerating plumbers who show up late, dress like slobs, and don't get the job done. |
| Stop being bored with.... | | Stop being bored with the same old pizza. |
| Don't miss your opportunity to.... | | Don't miss your opportunity to look five years younger. |

The above approach may feel uncomfortable. It focuses on problems instead of jumping right to the benefits of your products or services. It forces you to think deeply about why someone would part with their hard-earned dollars, as opposed to simply making an impulse purchase on a fad item. However, by starting with a problem that you solve, you have a much better chance of succeeding and cutting through the clutter of a crowded marketplace, especially in a world filled with skeptical buyers.

## TWO: WHO ARE YOUR COMPETITORS?

Chances are that there are other businesses already serving your target market. That's usually not a bad thing. It means that others have done the hard and costly work of testing the market and proving that there is demand. They have done this on their dime, as their unintended gift to you! Now you can study them to understand who is out there and how they compete. Then you can figure out how to beat them.

One way to assess the competition is by acting like a potential customer. Look at the *Yellow Pages*. Search online. Look in publications and other media where these businesses advertise. If you are thinking of getting into the retail or restaurant market, visit the businesses. Do some mystery shopping and get familiar with the customer's experience.

At the same time, think of yourself as a business consultant doing a research report to understand the market. Talk to industry insiders, like association executives, trade writers, investors, and consultants, and get their perspectives. Interview customers to find out how they perceive your competitors and the factors they consider when they make a purchase. Ask vendors for their ideas, too.

Answer these questions about your competition:

- Is the market fragmented with lots of competitors, or do a few competitors seem to dominate?
- Do competitors all seem to be about the same, or do you notice differences in how they compete?
- What products and services do different competitors offer?
- How do they price their products and services?
- How professionally do they present their image to the public, for instance, with signs, logos, the appearance of the business, and the professionalism of the employees?
- What products and services don't they offer that might be in demand?
- Which products and services seem to be especially profitable?
- Which products and services seem to lose money?
- How do prospective buyers learn about different options in the market and then make the decision to buy?
- Why do customers buy from these businesses?
- Why do customers not buy from these businesses?
- Which criteria seem to be most important when someone decides to make a purchase?
- What keeps buyers coming back and remaining loyal?

- What causes buyers to switch their loyalty away from one company and go to another?
- What are things that you must offer to customers in order to be competitive?
- What is each competitor famous for, if anything?
- What do different competitors seem to do especially well?
- What are opportunities to improve on what your competitors offer?
- Given all of the above, what ideas do you have to beat the competition?

## THREE: WHAT IS YOUR EDGE?

Of the five steps in this strategic planning process, this step is the most important and the most challenging. The more similar your business is to others in your target market, the harder you are going to have to work to attract customers. Therefore, it makes sense to identify at least one area where your business has a significant, meaningful, and unique edge. What will your business be famous for? How will your products or services stand apart from the crowd? What will you do better than the competition that matters to your target market? How would you fill in this sentence about your business: "Unlike our competition, we…"? The point of this exercise is not to match or slightly beat the average competitor in your market. The point is to set yourself apart as unique, distinctive, and significantly better in a way that matters to your ideal buyer.

Following is a list of different ways that many businesses use to gain an edge:

1. **Provide a great overall experience that makes people rave.** The Ritz-Carlton is famous for consistent, impeccable service. Their prices are high, but their customers don't complain because they leave the hotels and restaurants feeling pampered and totally taken care of. You don't have to be the Ritz to exceed your customers' expectations for service. For instance, John Hormighausen of J-BAR-H Texas Foods, LLC explains how he did that in the highly crowded BBQ market in Houston, Texas: "In Houston, BBQ is a commodity. The price of a

two-meat three-side plate is $9 everywhere you go. To top that, I am not only competing against BBQ restaurants, I compete against every guy who has a pit on a trailer and decides to call himself a caterer offering meals as low as $4 per plate. How to compete? I choose NOT to compete. We charge $12.50 for a 2-meat 3-side plate, and it goes up from there. We offer unique products that are relevant to our genre, but not common to other BBQ establishments. We have buffets that transcend anything anyone else is doing, and servers who are attractive and enjoy what they do. We take pride in serving even a humble hotdog. We are passionate not just about BBQ but about serving people and giving them an experience that they will not forget, as well as the best tasting BBQ they have ever had."

2. **Use your ability to innovate and come up with leading-edge products.** Apple, Nike, and Intel are all known for their ability to dazzle the market with new products that people want. In today's global, connected economy, you can come up with your own innovative product designs and have prototypes made up overseas within weeks. For instance, Darlene Tenes, founder and designer for CasaQ Ornaments has filled a niche in the overcrowded Christmas decor market by focusing on designs specifically for the Latino market. She explains, "When I was unable to find Christmas ornaments that I liked, I designed two hand-painted glass ornaments that reflected my Latino roots. They sparked an immediate interest from the Latin GRAMMY® Award producers who called and asked for them to be featured in their official celebrity gift baskets. Three years later my ornaments have garnered lots of attention because of the designs such as Our Lady of Guadalupe, Frida Kahlo, La Catrina, Pan Dulce and the Aztec Calendar. My designs are being test-marketed at 25 Macy's stores this season and are available at 70 museum and specialty shops across the nation. Some of the big boys have come sniffing around to get info from me now because they have been unsuccessful in launching a Hispanic line of products."

3. **Become a celebrity and expert in your field.** Design expert Kathy Peterson, developer of the Kathy Peterson Inspired brand, shares, "I made my mark in the crafts and home decorating industry by getting as much publicity as I could, making hundreds of appearances on HGTV, DIY Network, The Discovery Channel, and PBS, and by

getting featured in hundreds of big publications like *Woman's World*, *USA Weekend*, and *Better Homes*. I also hosted my own national TV series for 10 years, became TV spokesperson for several large brands and later became a lifestyle/design correspondent on Lifetime TV to continue building my brand. Most other designers were not making TV appearances, marketing themselves, or networking in other markets."

4.  **Satisfy a range of needs for the customers in your market.** IBM offers a range of solutions for the Chief Information Officer, their target client. You can do the same thing. Get to know your target market better than anyone else and create a range of products and services that addresses their needs.

5.  **Get your products and services distributed through unique or proprietary marketing channels.** Tupperware is the most famous example of a company that succeeded by finding a new marketing channel—in their case, parties. Similarly, when the accounting and consulting firm Arthur Andersen imploded, many employees started consulting businesses; their initial marketing channel was their former colleagues, many of whom landed executive positions in other companies. If you can find a unique distribution channel that your competitors aren't using, or can't use, you can compete. For many small businesses, one way to do this is through alliances. For instance, Mike Pacholek of Summit Assessment Solutions builds alliances with leading executive coaching program and human resources associations so that they offer his assessment tools to their members. That way, he brings a stream of business his way, while others help him with the selling.

6.  **Be better than anybody else at reaching and speaking the language of a specific niche market.** Monroe Baldwin of Myrtle Beach Tours explains how his company was able to tap into the student market for rental properties using this strategy: "We rent houses and condos in Myrtle Beach South Carolina, along with thousands of others. We found old houses nobody wanted to rent and customers to whom no one would rent: students. Originally we did all of our marketing in the student commons of a few key universities. Targeted school newspaper ads came next. Then we became pioneers using Internet marketing with our website and email lists. We continually learn all the new ways that

kids communicate with each other and infiltrate them to let them know we welcome their business."

7.  **Develop proprietary intellectual capital or technology.** When you create a unique piece of software or a proprietary training manual that other people value, you instantly set yourself apart as having something unique. For instance, a few of my companies offer a range of training programs for aspiring executive and business coaches. I created the materials for these programs after years of working as a coach and consultant and now offer them to others as part of a package of tools, processes, and worksheets. Once you have proprietary technology or intellectual capital, you can license it to other people and earn a stream of royalties for life.

8.  **Be more accessible.** Longer hours, convenient locations, and easy access to support can all set your business apart. For instance, Dave Greenbaum of DoctorDave™ Computer Repair shares, "In the computer repair field, I used our small size as an advantage because we were able to offer hyper-localized personal service. I could offer the same technician to come out each visit, and we also answered our phones after hours, such as on nights and weekends, at no additional charge. When the other guys were closed I was open. Customers were shocked when I answered the phone on a Sunday morning at 6am... and I got the business while the other guys were waiting until Monday morning to check their voice mail or added after-hours surcharges to price themselves out of the business."

Similarly, as the Marketing Director for Boreal Mountain Resort, a smaller ski resort in the Lake Tahoe region, Jon Slaughter and his team have to compete with 14 other ski resorts, all within about a 30-45 minute drive. He explains how he uses the idea of accessibility to differentiate the resort: "We invested heavily into our snowmaking operations, allowing Boreal to open about a month earlier than any other ski resort. This captures the full attention of the skiing and snowboarding audience, giving non-Boreal customers a reason to give Boreal a try. The early opening also generates thousands of dollars in free PR. Every major news outlet from San Francisco to Reno covers the snowmaking operations, then the opening. Everyone loves a 'first' story. Boreal is on the tip of the tongue for Northern California skiers and boarders for the first half of the season."

9.  **Offer no-frills, but consistent and reliable service.** McDonald's and Southwest Air are both known for competing based on low-cost, no-frills operations. They have their operations down to a science and can train anyone who fits their culture to provide the same experience anywhere they operate. The advantage of this approach is that you can also develop a franchiseable operation. Once you can get your business to succeed in one location, you can develop systems and people who can run second, third, and fourth locations. That way, you can grow your company and beat out mom and pop operations that can't grow beyond a single location.

10. **Compete by creating a loyal community of supporters.** As social media becomes established, more and more businesses compete by creating a community of loyal customers and followers. Some businesses have made this their core strategy. Mari Luangrath, Head Cupcakeologist and owner of Foiled Cupcakes, shares that her online cupcake order and personal delivery service succeeds based on her social media community-building efforts: "We've effectively leveraged social media to stand out from our competition. Over 90 percent of our business comes from social media leads, and we've surpassed our initial revenue target numbers by over 600 percent. We're pretty pleased with this, since nobody had even heard of our company a year ago and we have spent exactly $0.00 on any sort of advertising or brand awareness campaign. We get involved in authentic conversations that people can relate to, like pop culture, shoes, weather, chocolate, travel, music, or traffic, and help bring awareness to other local businesses and charitable causes we believe in."

11. **Gain advantages due to scale.** Home Depot started out with the idea that a huge box store can offer lower prices below the mom and pop hardware stores and make up the difference in much faster and greater inventory turnover. WalMart does the same thing. Now many other business compete based on the same concept, including jewelry stores, pawn shops, bookstores, and shoe stores. Even if you are a tiny start-up, you can still develop scale using the Internet. For instance, a marketing consulting firm started with one employee, but the CEO developed a database of 4,000 marketing experts he could call on at anytime for almost any project situation that came his way. Starting solo, he grew

his firm into a $10 million business serving some of the top firms in Silicon Valley.

12. **Be the best at sourcing products.** If you can find a unique source of products, you have an immediate edge. Diamond sellers, cement companies, resellers of discount inventory, real estate investors, and certain manufacturers all rely on exclusive sources to stay ahead.

13. **Update products and services to match the times.** Sometimes you can gain an edge by going against tradition. My wife's company www.etiquettemoms.com did just that, by updating the staid, boring, and intimidating field of etiquette training with a more inviting, modern, and friendly version.

14. **Excel at rapid product testing and roll out.** Many young companies compete by rapidly testing new ideas at low cost and rolling out the ideas that work. This is easy to do on the Internet, because you can quickly reach a huge audience of people to beta test your products. The Home Shopping Network and various infomercial companies also use this strategy to quickly test and expand successful products. Before the Internet and cable television, entrepreneurs did the same thing using direct mail.

15. **Create new rules.** It is easier than ever for entrepreneurs to change the game by offering products and services in completely new ways. Microsoft did it when they bundled Word, PowerPoint, and Excel at a low price, effectively putting products like Word Perfect and Lotus 1-2-3 out of business. Apple has done it with the iPhone. Zappos did it with shoes. TiVo did it with the way we watch television. Groupon has done it with coupons. Facebook has done it with the way we keep in touch. Google has done it with the way we search for information online.

16. **Be better, faster, and/or cheaper.** The classic entrepreneurial approach is to find something you can do better, faster, or cheaper than your competition. Pick any business, and you can see these principles at work. For instance, think about the national pizza brands. Papa John's claims to make a better pizza by using better quality ingredients. Domino's used to compete by promising to deliver a pizza faster than anybody else, until they ran into some legal and safety issues; however,

you can still track your pizza online and know exactly where it is in the cooking and delivery process. DiGiorno's Pizza competes on the lower price of its supermarket pizzas, while claiming to have the same quality as the delivery chains.

17. **Turn a commodity into a brand.** Frank Purdue and Orville Redenbacher are famous for taking commodities like chicken and popcorn and making people want to buy a brand name instead. Similarly, Mike Schwarz of RibbedTee.com is doing the same thing with undershirts. He explains: "We entered the crowded undershirt market and differentiated ourselves by: 1.) solving a particular problem—undershirts coming untucked and bunching; 2.) marketing our undershirts as ones you 'want to wear' vs. presenting them as a utility product like most other companies do; and 3.) creating the #1 destination on the web for undershirt-related information, and using it as a platform to expose our brand to the masses. Our company was cash-flow positive after 10 months and has grown roughly 75 percent - 100 percent each year as an online-only business since our launch."

18. **Bundle a more complete solution.** Customers want a complete solution to their problem, and many businesses don't go far enough. Offer support, warranties, ongoing training, free upgrades, follow up, and anything else your customers require to solve their problem 100 percent.

19. **Introduce a unique product line into a crowded market.** For instance, a baker in a major metropolitan area realized how hard it would be to compete in a city with so much competition among bakeries. To make his business stand out, he chose to offer the best desserts found all over Asia, including Hong Kong, China, Taiwan, Thailand, Japan, and Korea.

20. **Gain an edge based on your depth and/or breadth of experience.** Many consulting firms compete based on the depth and breadth of their experience. If you are going solo, you can still compete this way. For instance, Investigative Counsel Charles-Eric Gordon, Esq. writes, "I compete against less expensive investigative professionals, including private investigators and genealogists. The key to success in my practice has been highlighting the fact that I am an attorney, thus holding a

Juris Doctorate, with the critical reasoning skills and insight that my education and thirty years of investigative experience have honed, and as such, am familiar with evidentiary, administrative and other laws. This makes it more practical for attorneys and their clients to retain me over the cheaper competition, as I know what is needed and what can be done within the confines of the law, and it ends up less expensive for them to retain me over less educated and experienced competitors."

21. **Compete based on your selling process.** There are a couple of ways you can compete based on a unique selling process. First, if you are in an industry with a selling process that annoys customers, change it. That's what some car dealers have done with their no-haggle pricing. They list a value price for each car, and that's the price. No negotiations are allowed, and some customers appreciate the upfront approach. Second, online auction sites have revolutionized the selling process. Find something you want, make a bid, and either win or lose. Third, if you have the most knowledgeable and best salespeople in the industry, you can compete based on your ability to sell. Do you remember the home-based consumer finance company described in the first chapter? This company succeeded because the owner, a former banking executive, hired the two top-selling mortgage originators in the business to work for him in his home office. Almost overnight, he built up a multi-million dollar business; his salespeople did circles around the competition.

22. **Gain an edge with an exceptional product or service that gets rave reviews and exposure.** With a single outstanding product, you can compete. For instance, Gordon Ramsay's *Kitchen Nightmares* show featured a restaurant that was outdated and going out of business. However, they made excellent gravy from scratch. Gordon saw this and created a plan to make the restaurant become famous for their gravy. He launched a campaign promoting fresh gravy, including a parade around town that offered samples of the gravy, t-shirts with slogans about fresh gravy, and signs advertising their famous gravy. It worked. Similarly, a restaurant in my hometown has become famous for its turducken, which is a chicken stuffed into a duck stuffed into a turkey. They have been featured on a major food network, and people go there to try out this unique food.

# FOUR: HOW CAN YOU REDUCE THE RISK THAT BUYERS MIGHT FEEL BEFORE DOING BUSINESS WITH YOU?

Buyers today are cynical. Somehow you have to convince them that it is not risky for them to spend money with you. While it becomes easier to establish trust the longer you are in business, there are at least three immediate things you can do now to give buyers comfort.

**One: Provide proof that your marketing claims are true.** The more proof you can provide to back up your claims, the less risk customers will feel when they buy from you. Provide proof through testimonials, case studies of success, awards you have received, articles about you in the media, your own blogs and articles, your social media network, certifications, YouTube videos demonstrating your company in action, an interesting story about how you started your business, and free samples. In recent times, having a community of supporters on Facebook, LinkedIn, and Twitter is another crucial way to establish your credibility and, as noted earlier, can even be a core strategy to beat your competition who are not using those tools.

Even if you are starting up, you still can do all of this. For instance, you can get testimonials even if you have never had a customer. At a minimum, ask your friends and colleagues to write a few words about your character and commitment. Alternatively, as noted earlier in this book, hold an open house or give a speech and ask people to write down one thing they liked most about what you had to offer or say; that will give you a set of instant testimonials.

Davis Viera, who bills himself as The Real-Life Mentalist, writes, "I'm tenacious about building social proof, with loads of video testimonials on my website, high-powered listings on review sites, and an unparalleled guarantee, while other entertainers are too afraid to ask what people think of their shows."

Dave Hatter of Libertas Technologies shares two ways that his business proves its claims: "We now have nearly 50 testimonial letters, and they are a great marketing tool." Second, his company has also won a number of awards that add to his credibility, including US Chamber of Commerce Blue Ribbon Small Business Award, Cincinnati Chamber of Commerce Small

Business Excellence Award, Northern Kentucky Chamber of Commerce Small Business SUCCESS Award, and the Cincinnati Better Business Bureau Torch Award.

Derrick M. Guest, Founder and CEO of Griot's Roll Film Production & Services, uses certifications to get business: "In New York City, there are so many production companies that I needed a competitive edge. I decided to certify my company with the New York City Small Business Services and the New York State Department of Economic Development Corporation. Once I was certified, I was able to get small contracts and compete for larger bids and RFPs. Being certified has helped my business and built my brand."

**Two: Offer an ironclad guarantee.** If you really want to remove your customers' sense of risk, offer a free trial or a 100 percent ironclad, no questions asked, money-back guarantee.

**Three: If you don't want to offer an ironclad guarantee, offer an irresistible service pledge.** A service pledge strings together the promises you make to customers. Taken as a whole, these promises add up to a powerful, compelling statement about how your company does business.

---

## EXAMPLE OF A STRONG SERVICE PLEDGE:
### Mario's Plumbing Service

1. Our plumbers will arrive on time—not within a four-hour window, but right on the dot.

2. You will never pay a penny more than we quote you for a job.

3. Our plumbers have been thoroughly screened and background checked. We won't send anyone to your home that we wouldn't welcome into our own home.

4. Our plumbers will leave the work site at least as clean as they found it.

5. We provide a warranty that backs up all of our work for a full three months. If anything breaks after we have fixed it or is not repaired properly, we fix it at no cost to you.

---

# FIVE: WHAT WILL BE YOUR MARKETING MESSAGE TO COMPEL PEOPLE TO TAKE INTEREST?

Once you have identified your target market, the problem you solve, your unique edge compared to the competition, and ways to reduce the buyer's risk, you can create a marketing message that attracts customers.

Sometimes all it takes to have a great marketing message is a simple sentence that positions your business in a clear, unique way—also known as a USP, or Unique Selling Proposition. For instance, Shel Horowitz, co-author of *Guerrilla Marketing Goes Green: Winning Strategies to Improve Your Profits and Your Planet*, positions himself as follows: "I'm one marketing consultant who understands both green and low-cost." Back when his primary offering was in the local resume market, he used an equally simple sentence in a tiny *Yellow Pages* ad: "Affordable, professional resumes while you wait." He explains, "Both the affordable and the while-you-wait parts drew lots of inquiries, and the vast majority converted to clients. That was the only advertising I needed to do."

If you are not limited by the size of your advertising space, you can include a few other elements in your marketing message:

1.  Talk about the problem your buyers face and what it costs them. If you completed part one of the process in this chapter, you have already completed this exercise.

2.  Describe your solution and its benefits. Be sure to include the emotional benefits your customers will feel when they buy from you. How will you make them feel, look or be—young, rich, happy, famous, satisfied, peaceful, or secure?

3.  Explain your edge compared to the competition. You completed this exercise in part three of the strategic planning process.

4.  Reduce their risk so that they feel comfortable buying from you. This was step four of the strategic planning process.

5.  Have a call to action. Always end your marketing message by telling people what you want them to do next, whether it is downloading a free report or placing an order.

Following are some examples:

---

# MARKETING MESSAGE EXAMPLES

**Example One: Medical Practice Management Service.** Stop struggling to build your medical practice. Spend your time doing what you love, which is treating patients, and leave the tedious details to us. Our turn-key practice management service makes it easy for you to build a profitable practice, stay in compliance with the daunting federal and state regulations, protect yourself against lawsuits, and manage patient data. Join our service for a 30-day free trial, and if you don't see immediate results—while getting back in touch with the reason you became a physician in the first place—you have no obligation to continue. Click here to speak with one of our consultants and get started immediately.

**Example Two: Private Chef.** Sick and tired of the same old dinner routine? Would you like to have one of the most memorable meals of your life, prepared and served right in your own home by one of the top chefs in the city? Call XYZ Chefs right now and schedule a dinner experience that will be the envy of your friends and family. No other company brings top chefs right to you, so that you can reignite your romance, throw the best dinner party of the year, or sit back and relax for a change. We guarantee your satisfaction, or you don't pay a dime. Call now, before our chefs are booked on your special night.

**Example Three: Etiquette Training for Kids.** Don't let your kids suffer through one of those boring, out-of-date etiquette training programs. Instead, give them skills and habits that will last a lifetime, with a fun, engaging, and modern program. Your kids will have a great time, and you will be delighted at their new behavior. Unlike other programs, our teachers are engaging and focus on relevant problems like texting, Internet use, bullying, and peer pressure. Join thousands of parents whose children have enjoyed etiquette training with ABC Modern Etiquette. Call today and bring your kids to a free demonstration, so that you can see the difference for yourself. You will be glad you did!

**Example Four: Computer Repair.** Are you tired of waiting for your computer repair company to call you back and get to your house? ABC Computer Repairs has proprietary software that can diagnose and fix your computer directly from our office, or else we will get to your home within 30 minutes to fix your computer on site. That way, you can get back to work and stop feeling stressed out without access to the Internet or your work. Stop putting up with unresponsive computer repair companies who are condescending, confuse you with technical jargon, and don't seem to care about you. We promise to be on time, speak regular English, and solve your problem quickly and professionally, or you don't pay. That's why we won the Chamber of Commerce's Small Business of the Year award. Call today for a free coffee mug with our name and number on it. That way you have our information when you really need us. All you have to lose is your sanity!

Write down your marketing message here:

| YOUR COMPELLING MARKETING MESSAGE | |
|---|---|
| The problem and its costs: | |
| Your solution and its benefits: | |
| Your unique edge: | |
| Proof that your claims are true: | |
| Call to action: | |

If you have reached this point in the chapter and still aren't clear on how you are going to compete, keep working at it. It can take a bit of time to think through the different strategic options and make decisions. Sometimes you have to go back and forth between the steps before you come up with a strategy that will win. At the same time, as you have read before and will read again, you don't have to be perfect. Sometimes the best thing you can do is come up with an idea, test it in the market, and learn based on the results you get.

Once you have developed a strategy that will win, your next battle is to make sure your business will be profitable. The best strategy in the world doesn't matter a bit without a business model that makes you money!

## Chapter Five

# BATTLE NUMBER FIVE:
## Find a Path to Profits

A business that doesn't earn a profit isn't a business. It's a hobby. Some businesses, including big ones, lose money every time they sell a product, and they don't even know it. Your fifth battle is to make sure that you have a profitable business, not a hobby.

Some would-be entrepreneurs fear the numbers so much that they never go into business at all. However, you don't need an accounting degree to start a business. You also don't need pages and pages of complicated spreadsheets projecting every penny that comes in or goes out, especially before you have opened for business; that exercise will drive you crazy and probably won't be accurate once you get started. What you do need is an understanding of some basic but crucial numbers that tell you what your business needs to do to be profitable. Once you know those numbers, you can use them to set goals, track results, and take action to keep improving. This chapter shows you what those numbers are and how you use them to make sure you are starting a profitable venture.

There are four key questions you need to answer in order to be sure that you have a profitable business and win this fifth battle:

---

### FOUR QUESTIONS FOR A PROFITABLE BUSINESS

One: What is your income goal?

Two: How much do you need to sell to hit your income goal?

Three: What are the numbers that drive your sales?

Four: What does your income statement tell you about your profitability?

---

Let's answer each question in turn....

# ONE: WHAT ARE YOUR INCOME GOALS?

The most important expense that your business needs to cover is YOU. Clear income goals give you the chance of quickly matching and then exceeding your current salary and benefits at work. Think about two types of income goals. The first is what you *need* to make. The second is what you *want* to make. When you set your need-to-make goal, consider your current financial reserves, what your living expenses will be while you start the business up, and the milestones that determine whether you keep operating your business or do something else. Your want-to-make goal is a stretch goal. Set something ambitious, based on your aspirations. Fill in the following worksheet to declare your income goals as you start your business and then as you grow it over time.

| WORKSHEET: SET YOUR INCOME GOALS | | |
|---|---|---|
| Time Period | Minimum Goal:<br><br>How Much You NEED to Make | Stretch Goal:<br><br>How Much You WANT to Make |
| First Three Months | | |
| First Six Months | | |
| First Year | | |
| Second Year | | |
| Third Year | | |

# TWO: HOW MUCH DO YOU NEED TO SELL TO HIT YOUR INCOME GOAL?

Now that you have your income goal in mind, you have to figure out what it is going to take to be able to pay you the income you need, as well as the income you want. The way to do this is by calculating what's called your breakeven volume. Your breakeven volume is the amount of products or services you have to sell to cover your costs. Fortunately, it is easy to figure your breakeven volume out.

Every time you sell something, you have to cover two types of costs. First, there are the direct costs that go into your product or service. These are sometimes called variable costs, because they vary based on how many units you sell. For instance, let's say you run a hamburger stand, and that you only offer one product: hamburgers. Every time you sell a hamburger, you have to cover the cost of the supplies that go directly into that burger: the burger patty, bun, a few pickles, lettuce, a dollop of ketchup, a dab of mustard, a couple of napkins, and packaging. If you sell a hamburger for $1 and all of these items cost $1.25, you lose $.25 with every sale. In other words, your business is a hobby and you are basically throwing a big party for everyone in your town. If you sell that hamburger for $2.00, you have $.75 in gross profit left over. However, you are not out of the woods yet. That $.75 has to cover your second type of expense.

The second type of expenses are the fixed costs of the business, things like rent, utilities, insurance, ongoing advertising, telephones, Internet, and salaries, including your own salary. In the case of the hamburger stand that only sells hamburgers, let's say that you have to cover $50,000 of fixed costs every year. How many hamburgers do you have to sell to break even and still be paying your salary?

The answer is: Divide your fixed costs by your gross profit of $.75 per hamburger. You come up with 66,667 hamburgers. That's 5,556 hamburgers every month, 1,282 hamburgers every week, and 183 hamburgers every day, assuming you work seven days a week. You can figure out how many burgers you need to sell every hour or just during the lunch and dinner rush.

Now you have another decision to make: Is that kind of volume realistic? If you run the only hamburger stand in town, and there are tens of thousands of hamburger lovers in driving range of the business, you have a good shot; if anything, you need to make sure that you can handle the volume and have a backup cook on call. If you live in a rural community with a few hundred people, and there are five other hamburger joints within a mile of you, you are probably making a big mistake.

A second example of a consulting business shows how much simpler it can be to calculate breakeven when you are in a service business. Assume that you are going to start up a consulting business from your home. Your income goal is $195,000 per year. Based on your experience, you know that you can sell your strategic planning process at a price of $20,000 per client. Your direct costs are basically zero. That's because your clients reimburse you for any travel, document production, and other expenses. Therefore, you make a $20,000 gross profit with every engagement.

Your fixed costs are $195,000 plus the costs of your phone and Internet services which, taken together, add up to an even $200,000 per year.

In this situation, breakeven is easy to calculate. Divide $200,000 in fixed costs by gross profit of $20,000. You need to sell ten engagements every year to cover your costs, including your income goal. At this point, you have to decide whether you feel comfortable doing the right kinds of business development in your market to attract ten clients.

With the hamburger and consulting businesses behind us, here is the step-by-step process for you to calculate your own breakeven:

1. Start with the price of your product. If you offer many products, come up with an average price for now. You can refine your numbers later on.

2. Figure out all of the direct or variable costs that go into each product. Again, these are the things that you have to provide with each and every sale.

3. Subtract the price of your product from the direct costs that you pay with every sale. That is your gross profit per unit sold, sometimes called the unit contribution.

4. Add up your fixed costs. These are the costs that you have to pay whether you sell something or not. Be sure to add in your income goal.

5. Divide your fixed costs by the gross profit per unit sold. That is your breakeven volume.

---

## CALCULATE YOUR BREAKEVEN

Price Per Unit –

Direct Cost Per Unit =

Gross Profit Per Unit.

Fixed Costs ÷

Gross Profit Per Unit =

Breakeven Volume

---

Play around with different scenarios and see how your breakeven volume changes. What happens if you change your pricing? What if you cut your fixed costs? What if you reduce your direct costs? What is breakeven at your minimum and stretch income goals? What is your breakeven your first three months, first six months, and first year of operations? How does your breakeven volume change as your business grows and needs to add more fixed expenses to cover the increase in volume?

At the same time, do a reality check. What percentage of the people in your target market must buy from you in order for you to hit your breakeven number? Are there enough people in your target market for you to achieve breakeven, even if only a small percentage of them do buy? Do you have an operations plan that can produce that many units and provide reliable service to your customers, so that they come back?

For some of you, the work you do here will be a big wakeup call. On the one hand, you might realize that it is realistic to cover your income goal, if not more, and that you have a business that might actually work. On the other hand, your initial breakeven calculations might seem out of reach at this time, and you might have to do a bit more thinking before you make the leap.

Please don't obsess about your breakeven volume calculations. There is no perfect information. Once you launch your business you will probably encounter all sorts of factors, for better and for worse, that you couldn't have anticipated before you started. Use breakeven as a rough, back-of-the-envelope exercise to know whether you are in the ballpark or not.

# A PRIMER ON PRICING:
# 11 GOLDEN RULES FOR SETTING YOUR PRICES

One of the biggest questions people ask about starting a business is, "How do I figure out how much to charge?" Following are eleven golden rules to help you answer this question on your own:

1. **Your price needs to be high enough to cover costs.** Your costs determine your pricing floor.

2. **You can't charge more than the market will pay.** The market sets the upper limit on your prices. If the market will pay it, why not charge it? Research the market to get a sense of what other businesses are charging and what they provide for that price.

3. **Pricing sends a message about your quality.** People perceive a $1 hamburger very differently from a $12 hamburger. If you price your products low, you might unintentionally be telling your customers that your products are lower in quality. If you price high, customers might walk away, or they might think that you offer something special. If you do price based on this principle, then be ready to match your pricing with value, or your customers won't come back.

4. **Don't get rich on your first sale with a new customer.** One of the smartest pricing strategies you can use is to offer a product or service at a low price and use that to show your customer what you can do. This strategy doesn't mean you need to lose money up front, the way that supermarkets sometimes do with products known as loss leaders. For instance, if you are a consultant, offer to start out with a low-cost project that diagnoses the client's situation. After you assess the client, they will see the quality of your work and be more likely to hire you for the next, more expensive phase. Similarly, many infomercials offer you free bonuses with your first purchase. They want you to buy something now so that they can get your contact information and then convince you to buy a series of products over time.

5. **Raise your prices as you add more value.** My Center for Executive Coaching Certified Executive Coach program started out by offering a binder and a few telecalls for under $500. Since then, we have added five comprehensive manuals, a member area with hundreds of hours of audio lectures, worksheets, tools, one-on-one support, a seminar, and approved hours with the leading coach's association. Now the program sells for $5,000.

6. **Constant sales and discounts are dangerous, because they train buyers to expect them.** It is better to be consistent.

7. **Test, test, and test.** Frequently test out different prices and offers until you figure out what works best for you and your customers.

*continued on next page…*

*...continued from previous page*

8. **Pricing is only a piece of your offer.** Your entire offer includes your service or product, your company's brand and image, packaging, support, training, guarantee, warranty, your professionalism and integrity, your marketing message and materials, your visibility in the market, what other people say about you, and anything else that solves your customers' problems and makes them feel comfortable buying from you. If you make any of these more attractive to your target market, you can raise prices.

9. **Get over low-pricing-self-esteem and charge what you are worth.** If you happen to be a coach, consultant, or freelancer, then you know that your competitors charge rates that are all over the map—even for the same level of service and expertise. The reason for this wide variation is that some people have low-pricing-self-esteem and charge less than they are worth. If that describes you, get over it! Charge what you know you are worth.

10. **The more unique and rare you make your products and services, the more you can charge.** This is simply the law of supply and demand. By offering proprietary, one-of-a-kind, and limited-edition products, you can charge more because demand is high and supplies are low. That's why many direct marketing companies offer limited editions. Similarly, coaches can charge more based on how much access they grant to clients. They charge a low price for an information product with limited support, a higher price for group coaching, an even higher price for weekly one-on-one coaching, and a super-high price for the coach's home phone number.

11. **The more you create social proof, the more you can charge.** Fashion companies fight each other to get Hollywood celebrities to wear their clothes at red carpet events. Authors pay tens of thousands of dollars to publicity firms that can get them on *Oprah* or the *Today Show*. New York delis clutter their walls with autographed photos of the celebrities who have eaten there. Social proof also includes your testimonials, awards, case studies, certifications, social media community, formal credentials, and articles written by and about you. All of these things make people believe that you are the real deal and offer something special. They also allow you to charge more.

# THREE: WHAT ARE THE NUMBERS THAT DRIVE YOUR SALES?

Your third step in finding a path to profits is to understand the numbers that have the biggest impact on your sales. In every business, some numbers have a huge impact on results. They are like levers in physics: If you change those numbers by a little, they change your sales by a lot. These are the numbers that you need to track, review, and improve so that you achieve the sales you need to break even or better. To use a bit of business jargon, these numbers all create your revenue model.

What are the numbers that drive your sales? It depends on your unique business. For instance, my management consulting business has a fairly straightforward revenue model, one that many businesses can use, as well. In a moment, I am going to share with you the key numbers that drive my sales as a consultant. However, before you read further, note that I am going to share with you some real numbers, in order to give you specific examples. Don't panic when you read these! Don't think that you are supposed to know your numbers in the same detail! You are starting out, while I have been at my business for over a decade. For this reason, you won't have as much certainty as I do about the percentage of leads you can convert, how much money your customers spend on every transaction, and how many times every year that customers will buy from you. It takes time and experience—and a tracking system—to figure all of that out. However, what you can do is play with the numbers, look at different possibilities, and make sure your goals are realistic. At a minimum, you can estimate how many customers you need to hit your income goal. You can also enlist successful people who are in the industry to give you advice about your numbers. In other words, relax when you read the following information. Use the numbers I provide as examples only, not as an expectation that you have the same certainty I do.

With that warning, here are the key numbers that drive revenue in my business and probably apply to yours:

- **Number and type of business development activities.** These are the various ways that I get visible in my target markets, including speaking, leading seminars, writing articles, and asking for referrals from clients and the people in my network.

- **Conversion to leads.** Each of the above activities generates a certain number of leads for me, just like clockwork. For instance, I know that if I give a three-hour seminar to 25 people, I will get anywhere from zero to five leads, and the average is two. I know that if I meet with my network of ten top contacts at least once every quarter, I can count on one new lead from each. I know that every ten articles I write online results in a lead.

- **Conversion to clients.** Some leads become clients and some don't. In my case, about two-thirds of the leads who reach out to me eventually become clients. That number is higher for leads that are referred my way and lower for leads that come through the Internet. However, on average, I have a 66 percent conversion rate.

- **Average size of an engagement.** A typical engagement with a client is $20,000.

- **Average number of engagements per year per client.** A typical client will end up hiring me for two total engagements every year.

Given the above numbers, I can create a formula that sets goals for, and accurately predicts, my revenue each and every year. Let's say I want to earn $800,000 in a given year. Based on my action plan to develop business, I know that I can get 30 solid leads per year. So:

- 30 leads per year X 66% conversion rate = 20 new clients per year.

- 20 new clients per year X 2 engagements per new client per year X $20,000 per engagement = $800,000 in consulting revenue from new clients per year.

  N.B.: Because I have a business that has been going for some time, I can also add in projected revenue from existing clients. That way, I don't need as many leads or new clients to achieve my goal.

You need to create a similar formula to predict your own revenues. That way, you can be sure that you can hit your sales goal, which in turn allows you to hit your income goal. As you build your business, this formula also helps you figure out what you need to do to control and improve your sales. In my case, I know that if I want to improve my sales, I have some clear options, which include:

- Do more business development, especially the tactics that generate the most leads and eventual clients for me.

- Test new forms of business development that might get me even more leads and eventual clients.

- Get better at the business development that I currently do, so that I get more leads per activity.

- Convert a higher percent of leads to clients, for instance, by getting better at having consultative selling conversations.
- Raise my rates.
- Sell more engagements per year per client.
- Keep existing clients even more loyal.

What about you? Which numbers drive your revenues? You might find that the above framework works perfectly fine. If you sell products, you can also factor in how many products each customer buys from you with every sale.

---

## YOUR REVENUE MODEL

Number and type of marketing activities per year = Number of leads per year.

Number of leads per year X

Percentage of leads that become customers =

Number of new customers per year.


Number of new customers per year X

Number of products that each customer buys every time they buy from you X

Average price per unit X

Number of times a customer buys from you every year =

Total revenues from new customers per year.

From here, you can add in projected sales from existing, loyal customers...once you have them.

---

Take some time to develop your unique revenue formula. Again, play around with different possibilities rather than trying to nail down perfectly accurate numbers. Make it a game and have some fun. Check your numbers with successful people you know. Then refine the numbers as you test, develop, and grow your business.

# FOUR: WHAT DOES YOUR INCOME STATEMENT TELL YOU ABOUT YOUR PROFITABILITY?

The previous three steps take you through a simple, rapid process and quickly tell you if you can win this battle. Why waste time with more complicated calculations until you are sure that you have a business that can break even and revenue goals that you can realistically achieve?

Once you are sure of these things, you can go deeper and learn more about how your business generates profits by developing and analyzing your projected income statement.

First, rough out an income statement for your first weeks, months, and year in business. An income statement takes you from sales to variable and fixed costs to profits. You already have estimated your sales, your direct costs, and your fixed costs, and so it is not hard for you to turn that information into an income statement. Think about all of the things you will need in place in order to run your business, hit your sales goals, and meet customer expectations…and what those things will cost.

The formula below shows you an income statement at the highest level. Expand each of the line items shown so that you include everything that goes into sales, direct costs, and fixed costs. Once again, if you need it, get help—for instance, from your local SCORE volunteer or a friend who happens to have an accounting background.

---

## YOUR INCOME STATEMENT

Sales - Direct costs, A.K.A. cost of goods sold = Gross profit.

Gross profit - Fixed costs, including your salary = Pre-tax profit.

Pre-tax profit - Corporate taxes, if any = Net profit.

---

Second, after you have roughed out your income statement, do a double check. Be as sure as you can be that your numbers match up with how you are actually going to attract customers, make your products, deliver your services, and do what you say you do in your marketing materials.

Anyone can make a lazy guess. Your task is to make sure that your numbers reflect what is actually going to happen in your business. If you intend to attract customers to your website using Google Adwords, a social media consultant, and a search engine optimization firm, then those costs had better be included in your expenses. If you are selling a fruit juice that competes by having the best-quality ingredients, then your direct costs should be higher than if you were diluting your product with lots of water and sugar. If you need to hire contractors to pack and ship products, make sure they are included in your costs. If you plan on hiring employees, include your share of payroll taxes and any benefits you will offer. Get as much advice as you can from other businesspeople and consultants who know your industry and can be a sounding board for you. Get real quotes from vendors, and make sure they don't leave out any costs. Talk to leaders in your industry association. Visit your local SBA or SCORE office. Go in with your eyes wide open! You want to have the smallest number of nasty surprises as possible when you actually launch.

Third, turn the absolute numbers into ratios and make sure they are realistic, too. Expense ratios divide a cost into sales to come up with a percentage. For instance, if your direct costs are $10,000 and your sales are $50,000, then your direct costs are 20 percent of sales. You can do the same analysis for each and every cost your business will have, including rent, salaries, marketing, utilities, insurance, office supplies, and professional services. You can also divide your gross, pre-tax, and after-tax profits into sales to calculate your profit margins.

There are many ways to find out if your ratios are in range or not. Rules of thumb in your industry are a good starting point. For instance, for most restaurants, one third to forty percent of sales go towards direct food costs. If you plan on starting a restaurant and your cost projections are outside that range, you had better figure out what other restaurants are doing that you are not, or vice versa. Of course, rules of thumb are only rules of thumb. That's why you should talk to as many people in your industry as you can to determine how realistic your ratios are.

Fourth, project your sales and profits out over time. See how big your company can get, and how the numbers will change as it grows. Use a variety of different scenarios over a three-year period, including slow growth, moderate growth, and rapid growth. Set some goals. Plan for how you will handle growth and what kind of infrastructure you need to add in order to be able to meet customer demand. Plan for the worst, too. You have probably heard entrepreneurs say that it takes twice as much time and money as you expect to achieve your goals; make sure you know what that will cost you and that you can endure.

Don't obsess over getting these projections right, because you probably won't. The purpose of this exercise is to learn more about your business, make sure the numbers look promising, and to be as prepared as possible for everything—good and bad—that is likely to happen. Once you launch, you will probably look back on your initial projections and laugh, while revising them and continuing to get closer and closer to accurate forecasts.

The lesson of this chapter is clear: Before launching your business, make sure that you have a clear path to profits. By doing some simple calculations, you can be sure that your business is a real business and not just a hobby.

## CASE STUDY: HOW TO LOSE YOUR SHIRT BY IGNORING ALL OF THE ADVICE YOU HAVE READ SO FAR

Here is a case study from my own career, and I hope you can learn from it. It shows why you should really think hard about the issues raised in this and the preceding chapters.

Usually, I don't start a business that will cost me more than $2,500 to get up and running, and then only if it has the potential of generating 100 times those start-up costs in profits. However, for one very stupid moment in my career, I started a business that was a disaster. Had I taken my own advice in this and preceding chapters, I never would have started it up.

The business was a mixed martial arts, or MMA, fighting league. At the time, MMA was a booming business and the Ultimate Fighting Championship, or UFC, was just bursting onto the scene. I thought that, with the right concept, I could sell television rights or get into pay-per-view sales and make a fortune just like the people at the UFC were starting to do.

Take a look at the numbers with me:

The average ticket for my event cost $25. There were no direct costs, as every dollar from ticket sales went straight to covering the costs of the event.

The fixed costs to promote a fight included fees to the Florida State Boxing Commission and their staff of judges and physicians, arena rental, insurance, fighter purse, fighter travel, video recording and production, ring rental, lighting rental, advertising, program production, security, and some contract labor to sell and collect tickets. I calculated that it took $60,000 to put on my first fight.

Notice that I didn't include my own salary in the above number. I just wanted to get my feet wet and show that I could put on a profitable fight, and I was happy to take any profits after other fixed costs were covered. That was a big mistake but, as you will soon read, not my biggest by far.

I figured that my breakeven without my salary was $60,000 divided by $25 per ticket, or 2,400 tickets sold. The arena held 3,000 people. In other words, I needed to fill the arena to 80 percent capacity just to break even. I should have stopped right there, because selling 80 percent of an arena with a first-time event is unlikely, especially in a business where half of all tickets sales happen—or don't happen—the day of the show. Also, it turns out that I had to give away quite a few comp tickets to fighters and their families, and to radio stations for contests. That limited my upside even more. But I really wanted to give the business a go, and I was betting on the chance that I'd be able to create something so good that I could make money from television and pay-per-view, and so I put on the event.

The good news was that I sold out the arena. The bad news was that... well, there was lots of bad news. First, I spent way more than I had budgeted. I overspent on advertising, and don't even get me started on what you have to go through to replace fighters who drop out at the last minute. I lost thousands of dollars that night, even with a full house and some money from sponsors.

The second piece of bad news is that, thanks to the sell-out, I got cocky. I figured that I could become profitable...if only I had a bigger arena. So I promoted the next event at an even bigger, more expensive arena in a city about 50 miles away. I increased my budget on video production, thinking that I could use high-quality footage to sell television rights or get ready for pay per view. This second event bombed, for all sorts of reasons. We sold only 1,500 tickets at an average price of $20 per ticket. I lost my shirt on that event and quit soon after.

I never needed to lose all of that money. The breakeven analysis, plus some strategic thinking with a rational instead of star-struck head, would have saved me a lot of time, money, and aggravation. The breakeven numbers showed that I needed to sell an improbable number of tickets at each and every event to cover my expenses—before even paying myself. To make enough to hit my income goals, I pretty much needed each event to sell out.

Strategically, I compared myself to the leader in the industry. However, I was really competing with other local fight promoters and was too blind to see that. I had a unique team fighting concept, but we still used the same fighters and put on similar types of events. Looking back, there was no way I was going to offer anything compelling enough to get television or pay-per-view revenues, not without an investment of millions of dollars while I built up the business.

At the same time, I didn't have much control over my business. The Florida Boxing Commission almost shut down my first event because there was some sort of chemical smell coming from one of the locker rooms. Fighters dropped out of the fight at the last minute. Half of ticket sales came on the day of the event: Bad weather, a competing event, or an accident on the highway could have ruined everything at the last minute.

Finally, I really had no business getting into this business. People tried to tell me this, and I didn't listen to them. I knew some local fighters and fight promoters, as well as a major agent for some well-known fighters, and they all told me, "If you want to lose money, get into the fight promotion business." A major investor told me five reasons why he wouldn't invest and why my business wouldn't work. The owner of a local cable television station focused on fighting told me I was being foolhardy. I didn't listen to any of these people because—ignoring one of the mindsets you read about already—I wasn't open to their advice or help. The bottom line is that I knew nothing about fight promotion and made lots of rookie mistakes. To do it right, I should have shadowed a local, profitable promoter and learned the tricks of the trade before jumping in.

If there is a silver lining to the story, it is that I got to have a great life experience, and my family came closer together while I almost took our financial situation to the brink. Also, this experience has caused me to become totally, forever focused on businesses that I can start for under $2,500, so that I always keep my downside risk low. But I never should have gotten into this business!

Remember that the wise man learns from the mistakes of others. I hope this case study keeps you from repeating my mistakes.

## Chapter Six

# BATTLE NUMBER SIX:
## Generate Enough Cash to Give Yourself a Chance

The last chapter showed you how to find a path to profits. Unfortunately, profits alone are not sufficient. Many profitable businesses have died an untimely death because the owners couldn't come up with enough cash to keep them going. Meanwhile, many unprofitable businesses limp on when they probably shouldn't, often because the owner has a steady source of cash and a big ego and wants to see the business continue.

Cash is the blood that circulates through your business. If you run out of cash, your business suffers a heart attack. If you can't resuscitate the business by getting the cash flowing again, the business dies.

Therefore, your sixth battle before you leave your job and start a business is to make sure that you have enough cash flow to give your business a fighting chance.

Before considering how much cash will go in and out of your business, evaluate the cash coming in and going out of your personal finances and how that might change once you start your business up. Venture capitalists ask two key questions about new businesses, and you should answer these in relation to your own personal finances:

**One: What is your monthly burn rate?**

**Two: What is your fume date?**

Your monthly burn rate tells you how much cash you use up in a month. Get out your last six months of bank statements and track every single penny that you spend. If all of your incoming cash stopped cold, how much cash would you have to spend every month to keep up your current lifestyle?

Go line by line through each and every single way that you spend money, from grocery bills and your rent to clothes, restaurants, gym memberships, cable bills, taxes, car leases, and private school for your kids. Take a look at unexpected expenses that constantly come up, too, like car repairs, home repairs, and visits to the doctor. What can you cut? Come up with at least ten ways to lower your personal burn rate. Sit down with your spouse, if you have one, and discuss ways that you can cut expenses further once you take the leap to run your own business.

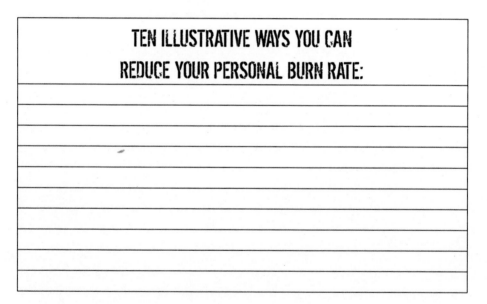

## TEN ILLUSTRATIVE WAYS YOU CAN REDUCE YOUR PERSONAL BURN RATE:

The second question to answer about your personal finances is: What is your personal fume date? Your fume date is the date when your cash reserves are gone, and your personal finances are literally running on fumes. If all cash stopped coming in and you didn't use your credit cards or other sources of debt, how long would you have before you completely ran out of cash? How would that change based on the ideas you came up with to reduce your monthly burn rate?

Once you know your personal burn rate and fume date, you can make some important decisions about starting a business. For instance, you might:

- **Stay in your current job and work on your business on your own time until you get it to the point where you feel comfortable growing it full-time.** Many consultants officially launched their business with their very first, paying gig. In my own case, I coached clients by phone at night and led strategic retreats for clients on weekends until I had a good stable of paying clients willing to refer business my way, and I felt comfortable going out full-time on my own. Likewise, online entrepreneurs often wait until they develop a website that's a proven hit, and then they jump ship from their employer to work on it full-time.

- **Ask your boss if you can shift from full-time to part-time employment, so that you have more time to build your business**. For instance, Ada Vaughan started her fashion-forward cloth diaper business CuteyBaby this way. She gained the time to launch her business, while still bringing in income and keeping her health insurance, by negotiating a deal with her boss. She explains, "When I realized I wanted to start my own company, I told my boss that I wanted to quit half my job. I suggested that for two or three days a week I'd work on my own stuff. He was very open to the idea. I took a 50% pay cut and worked both for my employer and on my own for a year. That way, I kept my health insurance and was able to pay the bills. Most small companies will entertain this idea if you have been loyal and productive—assuming your startup is non-competitive."

- **Wait to get started.** You might need to wait until certain unavoidable expenses—like medical bills or tuition for your kids—are paid. Set a goal, give yourself a deadline, and create a savings plan to hit your goal. Then dive in full force!

- **Use other people's money to provide funding.** Friends, angel investors, potential suppliers to your business, and even your employer might all step in to help you get started…if you ask. For instance, you already read about Patricia Kilgore in the introduction of this book. When her CEO told her to outsource her department, she used that as an opportunity to run it herself and start her company—with her former employer becoming her first client.

- **Sell something valuable that you own for cash.** If you are totally passionate about starting your business, you won't mind selling a luxury asset you don't need, like your boat, vacation home, or season tickets to the Bears. You can also downsize, for instance, by selling your home and renting, or buying a less expensive condo. However, make sure your family is on board before you do this.

- **Make a contract with yourself and your family based on the reality of your situation.** For instance, agree that if you don't get your business profitable and generating a certain amount of income by a certain date, you will find other ways to support yourself and your loved ones. Robin Barr, President of Cold Sores Begone™ and Canker Sores Begone™, did this, and it eventually worked out: "I started my business with X amount of savings and made the decision that if my savings went down to $20,000 and I wasn't yet financially self-sustaining, I would get a part-time job. After two years of hard work, that day came. I was lucky because I immediately found a part-time job close to home and, though underemployed, I had flexible hours and could continue to work on my business. After one year, the business had grown and I was able to quit the job. My self-esteem soared, not just because the business had grown, but more so because I had done what was necessary to keep it afloat and growing for the time required—one very long year."

Of course, you can always make some choices that many consider to be irresponsible: Max out your credit cards to cover your living expenses. Stop paying your rent or mortgage until you get evicted or face foreclosure—and then deal with having a horrible credit record. Raid your retirement savings, even if you have to pay a penalty. While you read about the occasional entrepreneurs who do all of these things and make it, remember that you read about these people because they make for good media stories. In reality, they are few and far between, and the odds are that these strategies will only dig you deeper into a hole. Don't you agree that you can use your resourcefulness and creativity to build your business responsibly, without putting your future at risk?

After you know your personal burn rate and fume date, you can estimate the cash flow of your business. Your sales and profits, covered in the last chapter, only give you a limited view of everything that will happen in your business. Your income usually never matches your cash flow exactly and can be quite different, especially when you start up. The table below gives some examples.

| CASH FLOW VS. PROFITS | | |
| --- | --- | --- |
| **Event** | **How it affects your sales and profit...** | **How it affects your cash...** |
| A client hires you for a $5,000 consulting project. He agrees to pay half now and half when you finish the project. | You have just booked $5,000 in sales. | Even though you can book $5,000 in sales, you only get $2,500 in cash right away. Hopefully the client will pay you the balance when you finish the project, so that you can collect the rest. |
| You buy a new piece of equipment for your business for $3,000 cash. | The purchase won't show up on your profit and loss statement, because it counts as an asset on your balance sheet. Over time, depending on current laws, you can depreciate the equipment, which is a non-cash cost. | $3,000 in cash goes out the door. |
| You buy inventory for your business, for $1,500 in cash. | The initial purchase of inventory doesn't show up as a cost. Each piece of inventory only turns into a cost when you convert it to product and sell it. | Even though you don't see an expense on your income statement, $1,500 in cash goes out the door. |
| You buy $1,500 worth of inventory, and the supplier agrees that you don't have to pay for 90 days. | The inventory shows up as a cost only as you convert it to product and sell it. | No cash goes out the door until you pay the supplier. |
| A family member gives you a $2,000 loan to start the business. | This doesn't show up on your income statement. | $2,000 in cash comes in the door, and now you have a $2,000 liability to pay back. |

By tracking your cash, instead of only sales and costs, you cover every single transaction that affects your business.

Cash comes into your business mainly from these sources:

- Cash sales.
- Cash collections from customers who buy on credit.
- Selling an asset, like a piece of equipment or a building, for your business.
- Getting a loan or investment, whether from your personal finances or from somebody else.

Cash goes out of your business mainly from these sources:

- Paying vendors for inventory, supplies, and services.
- Paying salaries.
- Paying for other operating expenses.
- Paying taxes.
- Buying inventory.
- Buying an asset, like a piece of equipment or a building for your business.
- Paying back loans, notes, credit cards, and other debt.
- Paying dividends to investors.

There are two types of cash flow to consider before you start your business. First, think about everything you need to open your doors. What one-time investments in equipment, supplies, services, and labor do you need? As you write down your list, think about ways to be creative and get those resources without cash. For instance, Ray's at the Serving Spoon in Sarasota, Florida, is a wonderful French restaurant that has done very well without making any investment in equipment. Rather than buy all sorts of equipment, the owners rent out a diner called the Serving Spoon on Friday and Saturday nights. They make some cosmetic adjustments to turn the diner into a romantic restaurant, and they serve a Prix Fix menu featuring some great food by an acclaimed chef. Instead of investing a ton of cash into a new facility, these entrepreneurs used Guerrilla creativity and agility to get their business up and running.

Similarly, I am in the middle of an exciting start-up that would normally cost me about $50,000 in web development and design expenses to get off the ground. However, my web developer and I have built up a great relationship over the past few years, and we trust each other. She has agreed to do all of the required design, development, maintenance, and hosting of this new website at no cost for the first year. In exchange, I am giving her a small, but potentially very lucrative, piece of the business. My total initial cash outlay to get the business running will be the 11 dollars I spent to reserve the domain name.

What ideas do you have to make sure that you give up as little cash as possible to get your business started? Here is an opportunity for you to learn from yet another one of my business mistakes: For the very first web business that I started, my partner and I spent over $40,000 on a programming firm that, after nine months, barely got us the infrastructure we needed to offer our products online. Part of this was because the programming tools so readily available today weren't available then. However, part of this was also because we were novices and didn't know what we were doing when it came to building a web application. Now I spend less than $2,500 to get a website up and tested, because I focus on marketing my products first. Once I see that there is some serious demand, then—and only then—do I invest in infrastructure.

---

# THE TWO BEST BUSINESSES TO START IF CASH IS AN ISSUE

If you don't have lots of cash on hand and really want to start a business, there are two types of businesses that you can start with little or no money:

**One: Become a consultant/freelancer.** Almost everybody has expertise or skills that others value. Most people offer their expertise to a single employer in exchange for a single paycheck. However, this is more risky than having dozens of clients. If you get fired from your job, you lose your livelihood until you find another job. If you lose one of many clients, you only lose a portion of your income while you replace that client. Plus, your upside is unlimited, because you can build a firm by hiring or contracting with other people, marketing information products,

*continued on next page...*

*...continued from previous page*

writing books, creating subscription programs, doing group and one-on-one coaching, licensing your content to others, and developing automated services. You need almost zero cash to get started as a consultant/freelancer, and your ongoing expenses are limited to your own salary. To succeed, you need to write a compelling marketing message about the value you provide, and then get visible in low-cost ways that attract clients to you. Ways to attract clients include referrals, getting involved in associations that serve your target market, speaking, writing articles, using freelance sites like elance.com and guru.com, and building your social media presence. From there, you can develop proprietary intellectual capital based on your work with clients, and turn that into a stream of products and repeatable programs.

**Two: Start a local service business.** Time-starved consumers and businesses pay for all sorts of services: hair cutting, landscaping, pool maintenance, cleaning, tutoring, piano lessons, art classes, etiquette training, cooking meals, child care, wedding planning, home organizing, painting, handyman services, home health care, fitness training, computer repair, personal shopping, dress making, interior painting, and more. Check your local *Yellow Pages* for ideas. These types of businesses usually don't cost much money at all to get into, because they don't need expensive equipment or start-up supplies. They also don't cost much to keep running, because they don't need inventory, a fancy office, or storage space. Once again, it comes down to your ability to develop a unique marketing message and then hustle to attract business.

Before you commit to spending a single penny to get your business up and running, think about every single way you can launch your business with the least amount of cash, especially cash laid out by YOU. How can you:

- Hire unpaid interns instead of paid employees or contractors?

- Buy inventory on a consignment basis?

- Extend payments out as long as humanly possible, or pay in no-interest installments?

- Get friends to volunteer their time and expertise?

- Test your product out before committing to a huge inventory order?

- Get your equipment at low cost by buying from defunct businesses?

- Get orders from customers before you order inventory?

- Work from home, without buying any new office equipment or fancy desks and chairs?

- Buy used equipment?

- Lease instead of buy?
- Get some sales and prove that your concept makes sense, before committing to developing a costly infrastructure?
- Get a partner to commit to funding part or all of the start-up expenses while you work for sweat equity?
- Raise money from others?

Once you have your start-up expenses listed, get comfortable with the likely flow of cash in and out of your business over the first few months and the first year. You already have some of the numbers you need, based on your work from the previous chapter. Now you can plug those numbers into your cash-flow estimates, using the formula that follows. As you build your cash flow projection, include other cash transactions that don't count as sales or costs. You want to include every single transaction where cash comes in or goes out of your business.

---

## YOUR CASH FLOW FORMULA

Cash In During the Period:

Starting cash that you will to contribute to the business +

Cash from sales, less bad debt and returns +

Cash from selling business assets like property and equipment +

Cash from investors besides yourself +

Cash from creditors in the form of debt =

Total Cash In.

*continued on next page…*

---

*...continued from previous page*

Cash Out During the Period:

Cash for operating expenses +

Cash for inventory +

Cash for equipment +

Cash to buy property, if applicable +

Cash to pay back creditors =

Total Cash Out.

Starting Cash + Total Cash In - Total Cash Out = Ending Cash.

---

How does your starting cash compare with your ending cash after the first week, month, quarter, six months, and year? Will you have enough cash to keep the business running, or is your business—along with your personal finances—at serious risk if you don't change your plan? At what point does your cash flow become positive and start to go up? How much total cash is needed for you to reach this point, including your initial investment to get the business up and running? When might you need extra cash for payroll, inventory purchases, equipment purchases, and other investments? How much cash does your business burn every month? What is the fume date of the business, if sales never come in? How can you lower your burn rate and lengthen the fume date while you get the business on its feet?

As you look over the numbers, think about ways to increase cash coming in and decrease cash going out. In addition to the ideas offered earlier, how can you:

- Get favorable payment terms from your suppliers?
- Get your customers to pay up front, for instance, with a discount for immediate cash payment?
- Keep your fixed costs and overhead to a minimum by operating at the bare-bones minimum until you get traction?
- Use free and low-cost Guerrilla Marketing strategies to attract customers, instead of traditional and costly advertising and marketing?
- Hire contractors on a project basis instead of full-time employees?
- Pay any sales people 100 percent commission instead of salary?

- Find a supplier who can provide small minimum orders, the way that digital printers can now print a single book for self-publishers?

- Negotiate payment arrangements so that your suppliers and contractors get paid only if and when customers pay you?

- Get unsecured credit to responsibly borrow money?

As recommended in the previous chapter, get as many people as you can to look over your estimates with you. They can make an objective evaluation, challenge your assumptions, and help you consider things that you might have missed. They can also help you come up with ideas to bootstrap your business and use as little cash as possible to get it off the ground. Again, speak to vendors, commercial bankers, SCORE volunteers, local business professors, leaders in your industry association, consultants, your accountant, MBAs, and anyone else who might help you better estimate and improve your cash flow.

When starting a business, you have to program yourself to imagine that each and every dollar you spend—in your personal life and in your business—is a 500-pound dumbbell. You want it to hurt when you hand cash over to someone else, so that you don't do it unless you absolutely must. Even then, you first do everything you can to legally and ethically get what you need without burning cash now or ever—without signing away control of your business by giving away too much equity. You are in a battle to keep every dollar you have from leaving the business, while enticing other people to let their dollars—or willingness to extend credit—flow into it.

This sixth battle tells you whether you and your business will have enough cash to give yourself a fair chance of success. If you can't find a way for your business to generate enough cash for it to be worth your time and investment, then go back to the drawing board until you do. Many, many entrepreneurs have started very successful businesses with very little cash, and you can do the same—if you use your creativity and aren't afraid to ask for a little help.

# GUERRILLAS SPEAK OUT WITH THEIR IDEAS TO SAVE CASH:

**Entrepreneur Shel Horowitz** started his business with almost no money. He writes, "Twenty-nine years ago, I started the home-based business I still run. Total startup costs were $200, of which $12 went to marketing, $12 for office supplies, and $176 for a very used IBM Selectric typewriter I bought at a school auction. I'm still home-based, but now have clients on four continents. And I still run on a somewhat thicker shoestring. Like a true Guerrilla, start with what you have and take the plunge. Get bigger later."

**Mike Scanlin, CEO of BornToSell.com**, shares: "The ways that I saved cash included: 1). The first nine months I worked out of the local library, because I didn't want to pay for an office. It was okay because I was solo at the time. I had no need to for phone calls, as I designed the product and communicated with outsourced helpers via email, using the library's free wifi. It was annoying not to be able to eat snacks while I worked, because no food was allowed in the library. However, it was very good for getting me to focus on the task at hand, which can be hard if you work at home, where there are distractions like the spouse, the pets, and the daily mail. 2). When it came time to get an office I asked around and found a couple of people who had an empty cube I could sit in. I had to move every three to six months, but it was better than paying $800 per month for a private office. 3). The real savings came from hiring outsourced providers online. Over 18 months of development, I hired around 30 people online for various tasks including logo design, web design, web programming, SEO, and accounting help. Mostly it was developers to help code the site. You can find good developers for around $15/hour out of Romania and Russia. Had I used local Silicon Valley developers it would have cost around 10 times as much. I also got consulting gigs through Elance while developing my site. I helped other startups with what I was good at—writing business plans and financial models—and then used the funds to pay the artists and developers of my site."

**Holly Landau of Landau Leadership** writes, "In our start-up phase, we joined a co-working space called Hive at 55 for $50 per month, instead of renting a traditional office. Second, we used as much free software as possible, like Survey Monkey, and free trials with WebEx and GoToMeeting. Third, we hired hired/trained qualified interns instead of staff. Fourth, we hired contractors for project work and paid them a percentage of the product sales on products they helped us launch. Fifth, we booked guest speakers instead of paid staff for webinars."

**Fitness trainer Andre Hudson, founder of Pro Builder Fitness, www. probuilderfitness.com**, writes, "I eliminated all overhead for my fitness practice by traveling from place to place. I run a boot camp in the morning at the beach or a park. I contract with a leading tennis center to train their elite tennis players. I visit homes to run private and group training sessions. I meet with professional and elite athletes on the playing field, to work with them on their playing surface."

*continued on next page…*

*...continued from previous page*

**Charles E. McCabe, CEO of Peoples Income Tax and The Income Tax School**, joined a trade exchange. He explains, "We became a charter member of James River Trade Exchange when it was founded and have used this as a way to preserve cash while also attracting new clients. Becoming a member of a trade exchange is a no-brainer for many small businesses that have excess capacity, which is true of almost all start-ups. Trade is especially effective for a sole-proprietor service provider because there is no cash used to provide the proprietor's services. A trade exchange eliminates the problems of direct barter, in which one party usually gets short-changed. It also handles all of the IRS reporting to ensure that all transactions are legal and the business does not get into trouble with the IRS. We have preserved many thousands of dollars of cash by providing our services on trade in exchange for trade dollars that we use to buy goods and services that we need from other trade exchange members."

**Julie Sue Auslander, President/Chief Cultural Officer of Subscriptions Simplified**, a minority women-owned business, advises: "READ, really READ your financial reports. By carefully looking beyond the totals, to the details, we cut out $30,000 of expenses without ANY pain. As you run your business, like moss on a stone, you attach unnecessary expenses without noticing. We had $10,000 in unnecessary bank fees, $1,800 in paper cups and plates, and $350 in credit card annual fees. 'Watch the pennies, the dollars will take care of themselves' and 'a penny saved is a penny earned' have never been more important."

**Adam Kruse, owner of The Hermann London Group**, writes, "Instead of buying desks from Sam's for $160, I found a hotel liquidator and got the same quality for $15. I was able to give my workers more desk space and still saved a ton of money. That helped out when I budgeted $30 for a lock for the front door and it ended up costing $511."

**Lee Zalben, President of Peanut Butter & Co**. describes how he shifted from an employee to a freelancer as a way to get his business going: "Before starting Peanut Butter & Co. I had a job with a good salary, great benefits, and a lot of responsibility. Once I decided to focus on starting my business, I knew there was no way I could do that and keep the job, but I was worried I'd run out of savings before my new company got off the ground. Luckily, I was able to use my industry contacts to score a freelance gig at an ad agency, working on a project that was expected to last several months. The pay was a lot lower than I was used to, but it was enough to cover my expenses. The hours were flexible, which allowed me to make my own schedule. When I was in the ad agency's office and waiting for feedback on the latest phase of the project, I was free to work on my business plan, do research on the Internet, use the phones, fax, etc. They even let me use their conference room to meet with suppliers. The project came to an end just as construction on our sandwich shop was beginning. The ad agency was happy to get my expertise on the project and I was happy to have an income and flexibility while I focused on starting my new business. It really was a win-win for everyone!"

## Chapter Seven

# BATTLE NUMBER SEVEN:
## Master Your Time

For many aspiring entrepreneurs, time is your biggest enemy. Many people just can't seem to find the time to get their business started, especially if they have full-time jobs and young children at home. Also, unlike money, time can't be replaced. You can always find new sources of capital to run your business, but if you waste time, it is gone forever.

This chapter equips you to master your time, so that you do what needs to be done to get your business off the ground.

The first step in winning this battle is to get grounded in the here and now. To do that, you have to abandon the idea that there is an actual date in the future known as someday. Many employees suffer inside their cubicles day after day, telling themselves, "Someday I am going to get out of here and start my business. Then I'll show them!"

These wannabe entrepreneurs are deluding themselves. There is no working calendar in the world that has an entry called Someday. If you are waiting for someday to come, you are wasting your time and part of your life that you will never get back. Worse, believing in someday qualifies you as slightly crazy, because you think that something is real that doesn't exist. It also sets you up to be completely devastated when you look back on your life and realize that someday never came.

If you are serious about starting a business, NOW is the time to get started. You don't have to quit your job or invest your life savings into your business. You just have to make some time to take a small first step, and then a small second step, and then a small third step. You can take that first step now or, at the very least, set a real date in the near future to take it. Now is real. An actual date on your calendar this month is real. Someday doesn't exist.

Once you commit to starting your business now, you have to make time. Even in today's world of all sorts of electronic devices designed to save us time and improve our productivity, we manage to waste lots of time. We waste time by sleeping late, daydreaming, sitting in front of the television, playing video games, updating our social media profiles, tweeting, watching YouTube videos, surfing entertainment websites, going to clubs, texting, emailing, going to parties, playing fantasy football, starting home improvement projects we know we will never finish, hanging out with friends who aren't going anywhere in life, eating snacks, creating unnecessary drama in our lives, hovering by our co-worker's cubicle, and getting involved in other people's dreams instead of our own. What about you? How do you waste time?

Before you make any choices though, find out the truth about how you spend your time now, by tracking your time using the worksheet that follows. All you have to do is track your time over the next week, in fifteen minute blocks. Every fifteen minutes, write down what you were doing during that time period. Use the worksheet that follows as a template. Don't fill in the other columns on the worksheet until your week is done. Simply write down the time of day and how you spent it, in fifteen minute intervals.

| TIME MASTERY TOOL | | | | | |
|---|---|---|---|---|---|
| Time of Day (15 minute blocks) | Activity | Did this have to be done at all? | Did it have to be done by me? | Did it have to be done as well as I did it? | Can I eliminate or reduce this activity to make time to start my business? |
| | | | | | |
| | | | | | |
| | | | | | |
| | | | | | |
| | | | | | |
| | | | | | |

| Continued from previous page. | | | | | |
|---|---|---|---|---|---|
| Time of Day (15 minute blocks) | Activity | Did this have to be done at all? | Did it have to be done by me? | Did it have to be done as well as I did it? | Can I eliminate or reduce this activity to make time to start my business? |
| | | | | | |
| | | | | | |
| | | | | | |
| | | | | | |
| | | | | | |
| | | | | | |
| | | | | | |
| | | | | | |

Once you have a full week's worth of data, go through each block of time. Look for time that you wasted and opportunities to stop doing certain things to free up your time for your business. Evaluate each time block and activity according to the four columns on the right. For each activity, answer with a yes or no:

- **Did you have to do that activity at all?** It is amazing how many things we do that are not things that truly have to be done. The more activities like this you can identify, the more time you can make to launch your business.

- **Did the activity have to be done by you?** Could someone else have done it? If you can get better at delegating and setting boundaries, you can find more time for other things.

- **Did it have to be done as well as you did it?** Often, we go for the A+ grade when all we need is a B. By doing things just enough to get the job done, we can save time.

- **Can you—and are you willing to—eliminate or reduce the time spent on this activity to make time for your business?** This question forces you to make choices about how you use your time.

What did you learn from this exercise? What are ways that you currently waste your time and can stop immediately? Which activities can you delegate? Which activities will you do well enough, but without going for perfection? What activities are dear to you, like family time, and what choices will you make about those in order to make time for your business?

Given your answers so far, how much time can you free up for your business?

## A BUSY MOM'S SECRETS TO RUNNING A BUSINESS WHILE CARING FOR THREE KIDS

My wife Elena runs a suite of very successful online businesses, including www. etiquettemoms.com, www.momsonedge.com, www.moneymomsonline.com, and www. artsandcraftsmoms.com. She knows a thing or two about managing her time, especially because she raises three kids from home while running the business and playing as much tennis as possible. Here are the things she has done to save time:

**One: Know your priorities and use them to your advantage.** "Because my business comes after my obligations to the family, I know that I have to make the time I spend on the business count. I can be super-focused on the business, so I can get back to time with family. I set a couple of hours aside right after the kids go to school to work on the business and make sure I get everything done that needs to get done."

**Two: Multi-task.** "Sometimes I have no choice but to pack product while also packing up my kids' lunches for school. Often I'm on the phone with a customer while caring for my baby. Multi-tasking comes with the territory."

**Three: Get help.** "Having my parents live close by is priceless. They are always delighted to watch the kids. My husband also watches the kids when I need to answer emails or ship products."

**Four: Use the leverage that the Internet offers.** "Having an Internet-based business is great for a mompreneur. People order from me around the clock, so far from 46 countries around the world. Working online lets me automate my advertising, email campaigns, and order processing. I still have to market, ship product, and respond to questions sent via email. However, I can do all of these things from my home, thanks to the Internet."

**Five: Set boundaries and priorities.** "There was a time when I felt like I couldn't say no to anyone. I had to grow a backbone in order to optimize my time—and act like my time is valuable, too. I've had to learn how to set boundaries and prioritize who gets my time when it comes to the business. I have to accept that I can't respond to everyone instantly. I've also gotten better at figuring out who is a serious buyer and who is looking for free information but will never buy—something that everyone with a business needs to know. Prospective buyers email me all the time asking me to call them back, give free information about starting a business, and train them for free. I'm very approachable
continued on next page…

*...continued from previous page*

and used to find myself talking on the phone for half an hour with someone—when others charge $200 per hour for that information. I've learned the hard way that serious buyers order right away, without asking for all sorts of free advice and information. So now I set boundaries and reserve phone calls for my best customers."

**Six: Do something once, and automate it so you don't have to do it again.** "I have an online member area with video demonstrations. Also, if a member asks a really great question, I'll write an article about it, post it online, and send an email letting people know they might want to read it. That way, I don't have to repeat myself. My whole business is based on offering information that I create once and sell again and again. I had to get over the idea that it was an injustice to each customer or prospect to not answer the same question personally, over and over again."

**Seven: Make sure there's value in it for your company, too.** "I get all sorts of requests every day from bloggers looking for free samples, startups looking for free advice, and entrepreneurs looking for me to offer their products on my website. They always talk about how I can help them but rarely talk about what's in it for me, too. Now I don't spend a minute on someone who can't show me how they can add value to my company. I'm trying to grow my company, too!"

**Eight: Use contractors.** "I save time by using contractors to design product packaging and book covers, help me with my online marketing, set up my social media campaigns, and manage my websites. The business is getting close to the point that we have to hire someone else to do all of the shipping, and I can't wait for that time to come!"

After you have done an in-depth, brutal assessment of how you use your time, take out a blank piece of paper. This time, re-create your schedule from scratch, setting specific blocks of time, on specific days, when you will work on your business. Simply block out the time that you have freed up and schedule it. For instance, block out time to work on your business while you take the train to work. While you watch your kid take laps at swim practice, set aside time to do a bit of extra business planning. Get permission to work from home a couple of days per week and block out the saved driving time and lunch breaks to get some personal work done. Wake up an hour earlier every morning to work on your business, and you will gain 30 extra hours a month. Go to bed an hour later and get another 30 extra hours. If you can't block out enough of your own time, free up time to hire a contractor who can do some work on the business for you, while you take care of your day job and family responsibilities.

Keep working at your schedule until you have found—and reserved—enough time to give your business the attention it needs for you to achieve your goals, on your schedule. You might have to make some tough choices. Your family might not see you quite as much. Your romantic life might suffer. Your friends might not call you as much, because you don't show up to hang out with them anymore. You might not get to work out at the gym as much as you usually do. You might take a pay cut at work to gain more time for yourself. Unless you have plenty of free time to spare, something has to give so that you can achieve your dreams. It is up to you to figure out what that will be.

Are you willing to win this battle and free up the time needed for you to develop your business?

---

# SPECIAL REPORT:
## Three Strategies for Time-Strapped Entrepreneurs

Let's assume you work full-time, aren't willing to go part-time or reduce your hours, and still want to get a business up and running. You have no excuse! Here are three strategies to use:

- **One: Do the work yourself, by moonlighting.** Even if you have a full-time job, you can still moonlight as a consultant, freelancer, or local service provider on nights and weekends. Many entrepreneurs get their start by moonlighting, filling up their practice until they can quit their job and go full-time. The steps to succeed as a moonlighter are: 1). Get clear on the expertise that you will offer, and to whom. 2). Craft a clear marketing message about the problems you solve, the benefits you provide, why your solution is unique, and proof that you are telling the truth; you can offer proof through testimonials, case studies, awards, and endorsements on your social media sites. 3). Attract clients through your network, sites like elance.com and guru.com, social media, articles and blogs that you write, an electronic newsletter, publicity, leading seminars or giving talks on weekends, and getting involved in organizations and activities where the people in your target market meet. 4). Deliver and delight your clients, and ask for referrals.

*continued on next page ...*

*...continued from previous page*

- **Two: Let the Internet do the work for you.** The Internet has revolutionized the range of possibilities for part-time entrepreneurs. Much of my own business income comes from online information products that run the gamut from boxing fitness and self-defense to sales and executive coach training. Other part-time entrepreneurs start websites that do everything from brokering vacation properties to offering local coupons to blogging in the hopes of gaining advertising revenue.

  You can also become an affiliate, driving traffic to your website and selling other companies' products in exchange for a commission. As an affiliate you never need to order inventory or ship products; the companies you represent take care of that for you. For instance, I sell some of my products through affiliates, such as The Fitness Training Company, and gladly pay them a commission for bringing me sales.

- **Three: Let contractors do the work for you.** The next chapter shows you how to build a virtual team of talented professionals who can get your business up and running for you. You can hire just about any kind of professional from anywhere in the world to do whatever you need done: web design, marketing materials, copywriting, sales, prototype development, manufacturing, shipping, accounting, search engine optimization, social marketing, and more.

## Chapter Eight

# BATTLE NUMBER EIGHT:
## Get Top Talent on Your Team

I t boggles the mind: You can work from your home and build a huge business with a virtual team of top-notch talent working for you around the clock, from all over the world. In my own case, my wife and I work from home and have a virtual team that includes manufacturers in China and Thailand; an on-demand book printer in the USA; graphic designers from Romania, Russia, Canada, and the USA; copywriters from the USA and Canada; Search Engine Optimization experts from India and the USA; a transcriptionist from the USA; editors from the United Kingdom and USA; and web designers and developers from the USA, Romania, Russia, and India. We take comfort knowing that we can live anywhere in the world with an Internet connection and run our business from there.

While researching this book, I met hundreds of entrepreneurs who have done the same thing. They have built virtual teams using some combination of local talent; freelancers from online sites like oDesk.com, elance.com, and guru.com; manufacturers from sourcing sites like alibaba.com; and providers referred through their network of colleagues and LinkedIn.

The first place to look is for free talent. Chapter Three provided a list of places, people, and resources—starting with your network—that might give you free advice and support as you get ready to launch your business. Review that chapter again, and make sure you have a group of seasoned, smart people on your side, with experience and knowledge that you value. At the very least, I strongly recommend that you create an informal advisory board, made up of people willing to support you; you can even add their names to your website to build your credibility and look bigger than you are. Also, form or join a mastermind group with other people whom you respect. Meet at least monthly with them to get advice and guidance, support one another, and expand your network. Finally, if your business includes providing a valuable service or product, you can barter for expertise that you need from others.

---

## CASE STUDY:
### Shaping a Business with Contacts Made at a Tennis Club

My friend David Morse had the idea to create an exchange that matched investors and buyers with banks looking to sell their troubled assets. He came up with a number of different revenue models, marketing tactics, and ways to connect the banks, buyers, and investors. To test and refine his ideas, he used his network of friends and contacts, starting with the many people he knows at his local tennis club. This club is not posh or exclusive by any means. However, David is well-respected at this club, known for being generous and honest, both on and off the court. As a result, fellow members were more than happy to meet with him and also connect him to others who could help.

He quickly got connected to the CEO of a regional bank, a successful investor in strip malls, an Internet entrepreneur who understands how to match up buyers and sellers, a number of real estate brokers and agents who specialize in short sales and foreclosures, at least two very wealthy private investors, and a few successful businesspeople who didn't know the industry but could provide valuable feedback nonetheless. By interviewing all of them, he determined the best way to roll out his idea and test it in the larger market, including what his marketing message should say. He also discovered the key objections that he would have to overcome from banks and investors, and the best ways to handle them. Some of these individuals even showed interest in becoming customers once he got the business off the ground. He got all of this information for free, simply through his membership at a local club and the people he knew there.

David shares some important insights based on his experiences with this process:

"I know it is implied, but the value of having a common bond of friendship based on something unrelated, like tennis, made the transition from inquiry to receipt of valuable information so much easier than a similar effort attempted with total strangers. There is such a comfort level—very valuable in particular when looking for the objections side. No one has a hidden agenda, no one is threatened, and the information you need flows so easily. Then the issue becomes to discriminate, to evaluate the info, keeping in mind the source, and the career and personal background of the source—all of which you know about, which makes the evaluation of the info that much more accurate."

*continued on next page…*

> *...continued from previous page*
>
> He continues, "One often hears that when you get something for free, its value is questionable. That may actually be true. However, in reality, the information flow we are talking about here, which may appear free in one sense—it is!—BUT, the truth is that one has invested a lot of time and energy in the relationships one builds and maintains with hard work, caring, respect, consideration...so there is a price of sorts, though it is surely an easy price to pay as it is natural and there are no immediate dollar costs to it."

After you exhaust your pool of free talent, get a good accountant on your team, if you don't already have one. Tax laws are complicated and change every year. You want to be sure you get every deduction you can get while you start your business. More importantly, when your business starts bringing in money, you don't want to have a nasty tax surprise at the end of the year. A good accounting firm has relationships with bookkeepers, payroll solutions, and retirement planning professionals—as well as with potential customers and investors. Look for an accountant who works with small businesses like yours, and check references. Early on in your business, you probably don't need much more than an hour or two of their time. Many accountants will give that time to you at no charge, in order to build the relationship.

Some aspiring entrepreneurs think that you need a good lawyer on your team right at the start. The fact is that you can incorporate your business at any time with a low-cost incorporation service, saving thousands of dollars on legal fees. You might even avoid incorporating until you have a few customers and know that your business is a go, so that you can spend those precious dollars on more important things like marketing and product development.

## DO YOU NEED AN EXPENSIVE PATENT OR TRADEMARK LAWYER ON YOUR TEAM?

Two areas that often get entrepreneurs swamped with legal fees are trademarks and patents. A trademark is a name and/or graphics that you want to protect so that no other business can use it. You can't trademark a name that is descriptive, like The Bagel Company or The Fitness Center. If you want a unique name, create something truly one-of-a-kind, the way that Google and Yahoo! did. Note that you can't claim ownership of a trademark across every industry; the trademark office forces you to

*continued on next page...*

---

*...continued from previous page*

choose certain categories that apply specifically to your business. Even then, once you have a trademark, you can still be sued. For instance, a company who was doing business before you but didn't notice your trademark application can still sue you once they learn about your business.

Start this process for free by doing a trademark search at www.uspto.gov and make sure someone else hasn't taken your name. Also, do a Google search, because existing businesses might be using your name without ever having filed for a trademark, and that gives them some rights. After you have done this preliminary research, and once you are sure you won't change your business name or brand, you can file an initial low-cost application to get the trademark process started and stake a claim. However, given how often things change in business, don't spend much more money on a trademark until you prove that your idea will work. In my own case, if I trademarked every business and brand name I've come up with, I'd be broke. I prefer to spend my money getting customers.

Patents are even more uncertain and expensive. It makes me sad to see entrepreneurs on reality television shows who have put their future and family security at risk by spending tens of thousands of dollars and years of their time to patent an idea that nobody will buy. Even then, as soon as they apply for a patent, they release their plans for the world to see, and anyone can make minor adaptations to their idea to go around patent laws. Therefore, before adding an intellectual property lawyer on your team to help you patent your idea, make sure you have a product that people want—and one where your technology really is unique! If you have investors who are willing to put hundreds of thousands of dollars or more into your business, and you have a $100-million-dollar, game-changing idea, by all means get the best patent attorney you can. But if you are not in that league yet, get a free consultation from a patent attorney to learn about all of your options and costs, especially the lowest cost ways to get started with some limited protection. Then ask the attorney this question: "Can you guarantee that you can protect my idea?" Once you hear their answer, you might reconsider spending all of that money on an intellectual property attorney.

---

Whatever you are trying to achieve with your business, you can find top-notch help, right in your own town or from anywhere in the world. This chapter shifts to two types of outsourced talent: service providers and manufacturers.

# HIRING A VIRTUAL TEAM OF SERVICE PROVIDERS

You can always find local professionals via referrals from people in your network and your Chamber of Commerce. However, local doesn't always mean better. Why not tap into the global talent pool and get the absolute best expertise at the best price? You can find these kinds of resources via referrals from your LinkedIn network and from freelance sites like Elance, oDesk, and Guru. Some entrepreneurs prefer to use talent from their own country of origin, especially for the most important work, while others want the best provider at the best price, regardless of where they live.

For instance, Jeff Bogensberger, CEO of SOCO Games, shares, "In developing our game, Earth 2.0, we used people in Canada, Australia, USA, Romania, Estonia, India and the UK. The amount of work that we were able to get was amazing for what we were required to spend. With tools like Skype and email, it was no problem. The risks of using virtual talent are no different than finding any supplier. You do your due diligence, ask for samples, and then hope for the best. Whether they are across the world or across the street, nothing changes. You expect to have an outcome delivered for a price. The only difference is that you broaden the reach for potential talent. We have had so much success outsourcing that it will be a long time before we bring talent in-house."

Catherine Wood Hill, CEO of Le Grande Dame, uses contractors from around the world to help develop and maintain her website www. LaGrandeDame.com. She writes, "I have found them in a variety of places, including oDesk and referrals. Our current website template was recently completed by a design firm that I found through a basic Google search. Once I narrowed down my search to the top three contenders, I requested proposals, and from there I checked references. The winning firm's references were impeccable, as was the proposal that they sent. To manage all of my contractors, I use a combination of Skype and email. I am very high touch and tend to respond to emails within a very short period of time and expect my contractors to do the same."

Catherine shares that she has been burned by contractors in the past, and so she uses three strategies to assure a successful project with a virtual team:

1. **Set communications expectations up front.** "I tell them how often I expect to hear from them, what the milestones are and when they are due, and how I want them to communicate. That way everyone is on the same page and I am not sitting around waiting on a response to an email for days."

**2. Have a detailed project requirement document that both sides have signed off on.** "That way, there is no question about what is in the scope of a project."

**3. Hold everyone accountable for deadlines.** "I won't put up with falling behind on deadlines, so I need my contractors to buy into the deadlines before the start of a project and to put some sort of guarantee into any contract."

Chelsea Moser, CEO of Solamar Marketing Agency at SolamarMarketing. com, chooses to rely only on contractors from the United States for her virtual team. "My contractors are all from the United States and I hire them on a referral basis, or after I see them doing work on their own for one of my clients. While I realize this may cost me a lot more to hire cream-of-the-crop virtual talent from the US, as opposed to someone I can find much cheaper on a freelancing job site, I feel that this is a must. I can't take the chance of hiring someone just to save a buck, if that person won't do good work. There are a lot of flakes in this industry, and when you have clients like mine, that operate on short deadlines, you can't take the chance of having someone falling off the face of the earth or not doing things right the first time."

She continues, "For anyone who's been burnt in this area, I say use virtual talent with a proven track record of producing good work, even if they cost a bit more. Ask for referrals from past clients and if you're using an online job site, take the time to read the feedback about them. It will actually save you more in the end, as you won't have to hire a replacement to clean up their mistakes."

Letha Davis, owner of Letha Davis Brand & Marketing Design, has virtual team members in Detroit, Texas, Oklahoma, San Francisco and New York. She also outsources some work to India and Russia, usually due to time and budget challenges. In her opinion, virtual workers are more motivated. She writes, "The biggest difference I've found between virtual and in-house employees is that virtual employees really want to work." Letha expands her team by relying on associates for referrals and by checking LinkedIn. She explains, "I've found that the people who take time to keep their LinkedIn profiles updated are typically career-motivated."

Katie Gutierrez Miller, CEO of Assistant Match, knows both sides of the business. She both hires and contracts out virtual support professionals. Her company is completely virtual, with employees and contractors working from their home offices around the United States. She shares that her screening process is "just like with traditional workers—interviews by phone, professional reference checks, criminal background checks, work samples, and test assignments, with the only difference being that we never meet them face to face. I learned quickly from my own experience that professional references are essential, and it's best to start small with projects in order to be sure the person is the right fit and so feedback can be given. People can interview well, so you need these safeguards in place to be sure the person is qualified."

---

## NINE TIPS FOR A STRONG VIRTUAL TEAM

David Hooper of MusicMarketing.com uses virtual workers on a constant basis. He is a top buyer on both Scriptlance and Elance, and a regular user of oDesk and 99 Designs. Following, in his own words, is his advice about how to recruit a virtual team without getting burned:

*The first thing to keep in mind is that, if you do enough projects, you'll get burned. When it happens, chalk it up and move on. To give you numbers, I probably get burned less one percent of the time. That's about five times over 700 projects.*

***One: Communicate.*** *Part of the getting burned problem is that buyers don't tell providers what they want. They'll say, "I need a 25-page e-book on dogs" or something that isn't very specific. Then they get mad when they don't get what they wanted. It's much better to say, "I need 10,000 words about training Labrador retrievers with positive reinforcement using the outline and notes which I will provide," and back that up by checking in during the writing process to see where they are and asking if they need any help. Providers aren't mind-readers. They want direction, so give it to them.*

***Two: Watch for plagiarism and copyright violations.*** *Some contractors may not be familiar with US copyright laws. They'll use code from established sites or images of famous people in graphics and company logos. They might plagiarize from other sites. These kinds of things happen from time to time, probably by accident. It's getting better. Programs like Copyscape can help to identify plagiarism.*

***Three: Avoid brand-new providers.*** *By working with people who have a history and good references, you can screen out the flakes. Let new providers get their initial projects from somebody else, unless you have a very small project.*

*continued on next page…*

*...continued from previous page*

**Four: Avoid providers who have had projects but no feedback posted.** *No feedback = bad feedback, because some people don't like to leave bad feedback*

**Five: Communicate on a basic level.** *Some of these guys don't speak English very well, so you have to be sure they understand what you need.*

**Six: Use escrow.** *Elance and other sites offer escrow protection. You pay into their escrow account and release funds when your provider delivers. That protects you in case something goes wrong. By putting 100 percent of the money in escrow up front, you also let the provider know that you are honest and acting in good faith. Providers are afraid of getting burned, too!*

**Seven: Treat your providers right.** *Providers talk with each other; if you're not honest and easy to deal with, they'll know it and you'll only get bids from boiler rooms who don't care about quality. ALWAYS pay/release the money as soon as the work is completed. ALWAYS leave feedback when somebody does a good job.*

**Eight: Build your reputation on the site by keeping your award ratio up and showing that you're a real company with a project worth considering.** *Some sites charge providers every time they bid on a project. By having a good award ratio, you get more bids. Providers know that you're less likely to bail on a project before it even starts, which is very common.*

**Nine: With all this said, in the end, you have to trust people.** *My experience is that 99 percent, or more, of people are honest. I have had some amazing experiences with people both in the United States and abroad. We work with a lot of freelancers and, depending on how we find them, sometimes there is no escrow available. Sometimes I pay 100 percent upfront. On these deals, I have never been burned. The majority of people are appreciative of the work you're providing them with and want to develop a long-term relationship, so they're going to take care of you.*

# AN INTERVIEW WITH ELLEN PACK, VICE PRESIDENT OF MARKETING, ELANCE

As Vice President of Marketing at Elance, Ellen Pack enjoys a bird's eye view of the virtual talent marketplace. Following are her answers to some questions about the trend in recruiting virtual service professionals:

**Q: What growth has Elance seen in solopreneurs using Elance to create virtual teams?**

*continued on next page...*

*…continued from previous page*

A: *Solopreneurs and small businesses are using Elance in record numbers to hire and manage online teams. Over 125,000 solopreneurs and small businesses have posted more than 400,000 jobs in the past year, up 40% over the prior year. More businesses are adopting the model of online work because it offers them access to top talent on a flexible basis. It's a low-overhead way to build a team and build a business.*

**Q: How does a solopreneur make sure they are getting talent and not just someone who presents themselves well but isn't any good?**

A: *Elance helps solopreneurs and small businesses find the best online workers available anywhere. The Elance online employment platform features over 300,000 online professionals, representing over 400 different skills. Every Elance professional has the opportunity to display their online profile, which includes their digital portfolio of work. Potential employers are able to browse their work samples, which may include graphic design projects, writing samples, coding or website screenshots they have developed. Elance online professionals are required to take an admissions test and have the option to take and post the results of skills tests. They can also opt to verify their credentials. Each worker's profile includes verified work history on Elance and direct performance feedback from prior employers.*

**Q: How does a solopreneur protect himself with payment/security?**

A: *Elance has a number of safeguards in place to help facilitate security and payments for performance on its platform. For fixed-price jobs, Elance's licensed escrow service protects both parties by guaranteeing payment for results: the work is pre-funded, but payments are released only when specified milestones are met and results are approved by the employer. For hourly work, Elance offers Work View™, which allows employers to see online work as it progresses and approve timesheets backed by screenshots for all hours billed. Finally, when businesses work through Elance, all work is governed by the "Services Agreement between Client and Provider," which covers confidentiality and intellectual property rights.*

**Q: How else has Elance changed the world for the solopreneur who needs talent?**

A: *Online jobs are not based in any physical location, so solopreneurs, start-ups and small businesses are now able to tap into the human cloud of online workers and hire specialized talent on a more flexible basis. At Elance, we are focused on building a platform to help facilitate all aspects of online work by helping match employers with skilled workers, building trust in the working relationship and focusing on compliance to help solopreneurs and small businesses securely navigate and thrive as they leverage online work teams.*

# HIRING A VIRTUAL MANUFACTURING TEAM

If you need to manufacture a product, be extremely thorough when you choose your supplier. It takes time and money to get a new supplier on board, and you don't want to switch in case your primary provider can't deliver on a big order or has constant quality problems. Even large companies have been burned by overseas suppliers producing tainted products, like toys made with lead or drywall that produces toxic chemicals. More common problems include constant production delays and inconsistent quality. While domestic firms might be more reliable, it can be very challenging to find a company that produces at a competitive price compared to overseas providers.

You can find manufacturers abroad through the website alibaba.com. You can find domestic manufacturers through Thomas Register and their website www.thomasnet.net. If you are new to manufacturing, get as much advice as you can before you jump in. Learn about retailer expectations, safety laws, customs duties, shipping options and costs, terms to negotiate, realistic turnaround times, packaging, and your legal recourse in case the supplier doesn't meet your expectations.

My wife Elena has manufactured almost a dozen products overseas for her company. She starts by creating prototypes in our kitchen, using materials that she knows will not cause issues with customs, have high import tariffs, or that have the risk of being tainted. Then she ships the prototype overseas for a quote; she found her initial suppliers through alibaba.com. She chooses a supplier based on the quality of the prototype, price, delivery time, minimum order quantity, and references.

While 90% of her suppliers have worked out fine, one in particular was horrible. He couldn't have been more charming when we considered hiring him. He said the right things, produced quality samples, and promised us fantastic quality within a short time frame. We needed the product quickly and made the mistake of hiring him without asking for references. Everything went downhill from there. After we sent him money per our agreed-upon terms, he insisted we pay even more to complete the mold development process; he refused to give us our initial money back, and it felt like he was holding us hostage. He missed the promised delivery date by months, with a list of excuses that made us scream in disbelief. Then he shipped partial orders, and we were never sure if he would complete the rest of the order—all while making our shipping costs skyrocket. Also, despite promising FOB, or Free On Board delivery, he refused to release any products unless we paid extra for him to ship product from his factory to the port, which made our shipping costs higher still. One box of products came packed upside down, and my wife had to unpack and repack each and every one. He even became verbally abusive in his emails when we complained. Fortunately, he was only a backup supplier, and my wife doesn't use him anymore. The lesson: Always get references! In this case, we eventually got a call from another of his customers, who somehow found out about us while on a factory tour in China. He, too, was experiencing all sorts of production delays—and this put him at risk of losing a $50,000 order from a major retail chain.

Ada Vaughan followed an effective process when she found a manufacturer for her fashion-forward cloth diaper business CuteyBaby. After she worked with a seamstress to make a prototype, a colleague gave her a referral to a manufacturing source in China. The source represented multiple factories, which reduced her risk. Also, the manufacturing company she chose had an American representative working in China, as well as a stateside contact. Ada made sure the company could quickly produce a four-to-six month supply of inventory, because big chains need assurances before they are willing to place a wholesale order.

She worked with the company to make samples, test them, and tweak them. She also got her product tested by an independent lab and approved for the Consumer Products Safety Improvement Act, which is required for baby products. She went into production with an initial order of 2,000 units. Now she is shipping product to major retailers in the United States.

Here is a checklist of eighteen key points to consider before going overseas with your sourcing, with thanks to Ada for refining and adding to my original list:

# YOUR 18-POINT CHECKLIST FOR SOURCING PRODUCT OVERSEAS

1.  You have tested your product's functionality by making a prototype or small production run and giving it to unbiased third parties to assess. For instance, in Ada's industry, mommy bloggers are a great resource for this. Once you are certain that the prototype has proven successful, then go overseas for a quote.

2.  You have a solid understanding of packaging requirements for your products. This can be anything from FTC fiber content on a tag to a specific retailer's needs.

3.  You have received multiple quotes for the same project or production run. Factories will often change their pricing depending on demand, so a busy factory may give you a higher price simply because they aren't hungry for the work.

4.  You clearly understand the quote/price provided and what payment terms are expected.

5.  You know how far in advance the factory is taking orders. Sometimes they may be able to get you right in, with a standard 30-day turnaround. During a busy phase, they may have four months of work on deck.

6.  The supplier has provided references that you have personally checked. Other companies have experienced excellent quality, timely delivery, and honest dealings from them.

7.  The supplier meets manufacturing standards for products exported to and marketed in the United States.

8.  There is a contact person who speaks your language fluently. Ideally, the facility has a contact who resides stateside.

9.  The supplier has the capacity to produce a four-to-six month supply of your product with a 30-day turnaround. This is a tough one, because a lot of established factories won't touch you when you are starting out. Be prepared to switch factories as you grow your business.

10. You have an agreement that you own any molds/dies/designs and that the supplier will store them safely and hand them over to you upon request.

11. The supplier has no history of using tainted products or materials, and you are 100 percent clear about which materials they will and will not use.

12. You have factored shipping costs into your cost analysis, including cost from factory to port and from port to your door.

*continued on next page...*

*...continued from previous page*

13. You have a process in place to receive test samples before full production. The manufacturer agrees that, if they go into full production before creating samples, they are liable for any errors.

14. You have a process in place to inspect goods before shipment. If you can't travel to the plant, inspect via photos or video camera.

15. You know how customs will categorize the product and what tariffs you have to pay. Be sure you have the correct Harmonized Tariff Schedule (HTS) code; everything is calculated based on that.

16. You know about any certifications and product testing required for your specific product.

17. You have secured a customs bond and/or are working with a customs agent or freight forwarder who will accept your shipment when it arrives. Be sure to get multiple quotes on freight. Quotes can vary widely.

18. You have put together a realistic production timeline so you can forecast your needs and order appropriately. Make sure you have the capital on hand to order the products you need.

## Chapter Nine

# BATTLE NUMBER NINE:

## Achieve Quick, Low-Risk Successes To Get Your First Profitable Customer

Almost nothing beats the thrill of seeing that first order come through online, hearing the first ring of the cash register, or getting the first signed contract from a client. This chapter is about winning that battle, so you can enjoy that experience.

By winning the previous eight battles in this book, you have already laid the foundation to get that first customer. For some of you, the act of getting out and talking to people about your idea will be enough to attract your first customer. Somebody might hear about the solution you can provide to their problem and want to hire you on the spot, or as soon as you are ready to launch.

For others, the battle to get that first customer will be a lengthy and grueling campaign. The initial phase of getting a business going can be like pushing a rock up a hill. You feel like you have to put five or ten units of energy into your business to get one unit back to you. You spend lots of time trying different tactics that don't work out, and wonder whether your business will ever make it. If your start up happens to go that way, don't give up. Keep testing, tweaking, and moving forward. Many would-be entrepreneurs aren't willing to do the hard work required to get that first customer and quit too soon—even if they are only a few steps away from success.

There are two ideas that are central to getting your first profitable customer. The first is the key number that tells you whether your marketing is profitable. The second is the testing lab, which lets you get that first customer without taking big risks. Let's explore both...

# THE KEY NUMBER THAT TELLS YOU IF YOUR MARKETING IS PROFITABLE

The key number you have to track is your cost per order, or CPO, sometimes called your customer acquisition cost. This is how much it costs you to get a new customer. Some tactics to attract customers, especially referrals and social marketing that you do yourself, are essentially free. Other tactics, like direct mail and traditional advertising, can be quite costly.

CPO tells you whether you are spending your marketing money profitably. For instance, assume that you spend $1,000 to mail postcards to a small list that you have bought. Ten people respond to your mailing, and two of them become customers. It cost you $100 to get those ten leads—$1,000 divided by ten leads—and $500 to get those two customers—$1,000 divided by two. Your CPO for that mailing is $500.

For some businesses, a CPO of $500 is great news. For others, it is a disaster. It depends on your gross profit per order. Gross profit per order is how much money the average customer spends on their first order, less how much your direct costs are for that order. If you have a restaurant and the average customer pays $10 each meal, and it costs you $4 in food and packaging costs to serve them, then your gross profit is $6. In this case, you would lose your shirt on a CPO basis if you keep doing a postcard mailing. That's because you spend $500 to get back $6 in gross profit.

On the other hand, suppose you sell cars, and the average customer brings you $1,250 in gross profits per sale. Your postcard mailing is a success. It cost you $500 to get a customer, and each customer brought you $1,250 in profits. That leaves $750 to cover fixed costs, including your salary. Put another way, the $1,000 mailing brought you a total of $2,500 in gross profits and leaves you $1,500 after the cost of the mailing—$2,500 less the $1,000 cost of the mailing—to cover fixed costs.

Some businesspeople would argue that the above analysis is incomplete, because it doesn't take into account how much your new customers will buy over their lifetime. For instance, in the current example, the hamburger restaurant would have spent $500 to get a new customer, all for $6 in gross profit from that customer on their initial visit. That's unprofitable, to put it mildly. However, suppose that this same customer comes back for lunch 100 times over the next few years, contributing $6 in gross profit every time. Now you make $600 for that customer. Suddenly, the $1,000 mailing doesn't look so horrible. Now suppose that each customer tells five other people to come to your restaurant, and they eat lunch at your restaurant 100 times, too. That's $600 X 5, or $3,000 in gross profit from the referred customers. The total $1,000 mailing contributes $3,600 in gross profits. When you take the theoretical lifetime value of a customer into consideration, the postcard mailing looks ingenious.

But be careful! While lifetime value is enticing, it is misleading. You can run out of cash very quickly as a start-up entrepreneur if you use lifetime value as your primary metric. With enough rosy assumptions about how much your customers will buy over time, you can justify almost any marketing expense. Unfortunately, you may be making false assumptions based on hope rather than logic and good business sense.

When your business is up and running and you have hard data about what customers really buy from you over time, you can incorporate lifetime value into your marketing. Even then, take care. The most profitable businesses try to attract customers so that they are profitable right away, on the very first order.

The Guerrilla tracks each and every marketing tactic to know for sure whether it worked or not. The rule is non-negotiable: If it costs you money, you need to find a way to track results. At a minimum, ask people how they heard about you and keep track of those statistics. For instance, when the Renaissance Fair comes to my town and we buy a ticket at their box office, the ticket salesperson asks us to fill in a survey about where we heard about them. They give us a half-page of paper listing everywhere they advertise— the weekly free paper, local paper, a couple of radio stations, their website, and word of mouth. That way, they know where to focus their advertising next year.

Similarly, one of the reasons Google has become such a profitable business is because it lets business owners track almost everything a buyer does and then make decisions based on that information. It tells us how often our advertisements show, how many people click the ad, how many sign up for our free email newsletter, and how many buy something from us. It lets us calculate the cost of each conversion and compare that to our gross profit. It lets us do this for each and every keyword, geographic location where the ad runs, variation in ad copy—and any date range that we want to select. Based on this information, we can pay more for keywords that are profitable for us, delete ads that aren't working, and constantly improve our results.

## THE TESTING LAB: YOUR LOW-RISK WAY TO A PROFITABLE CUSTOMER

The second idea that is central to getting your first profitable customer is the testing lab. Think of your business as a laboratory. You are the chief scientist, and your mission is to discover the formula for profits. Like any competent scientist, you start with small experiments, until you make a discovery that is worth exploring with a bigger test. Once you prove that an idea has legs, you can scale it up and roll it out.

By using this approach to attract your first profitable customer, you don't have to take big risks to get your business going. If you fall into the trap of thinking that you do have to take big risks, then go back to the drawing board. Think more creatively about your business, so that you don't have to spend tons of money or quit your job—especially before you even get your first profitable customer.

For instance, let me tell you the story of how one of my businesses evolved from a single web page into something much more significant. As you read earlier, I run a business that provides distance-learning fitness certifications to fitness professionals. If you went to my websites now, you would see six different websites offering ten different programs, from boxing and kickboxing fitness to innovative strength training, speed and agility training, self-defense, and nutrition. The company has published over a dozen fitness training manuals and accompanying DVDs and has an extensive online member area with hundreds of hours of video clips. We also offer live seminars. The various programs we offer are approved for continuing education units by leading fitness organizations, and we have customers and testimonials from around the world.

It wasn't always this way. Not even close.

Go back almost a decade, when I started taking a boxing fitness class and really liked it. The owner of the gym, Tony Spain, was a former professional boxer who was passionate about teaching people boxing fitness, and it was clear that he was many steps above the traditional boxing trainer. People of all ages and backgrounds loved his style and the way that he had broken down boxing fitness into a step-by-step system. I couldn't believe that Tony wasn't known nationally. I asked him if he would be interested in creating a program to teach other fitness professionals to teach boxing fitness, and he agreed.

After we signed a one-page letter of understanding, I took small steps to test the idea of offering a distance-learning boxing fitness certification program. First, I hired a web designer in India to create a single web page inviting fitness professionals to get certified as a Boxing Fitness Trainer. It cost me $250 to get that website up, plus $19 per month for a shopping cart service to process orders. I also spent $500 on a local videographer to tape Tony in his boxing gym.

As soon as this simple site was up, I used Google Adwords to test different prices, headlines, and offers. I spent a few hundred dollars on offers that didn't work but didn't panic when they failed. Then I tested a price that let customers pay in monthly installments. It cost me just $30 in Google Adwords to get my first customer at this new price, and each sale generated around $200 in gross profit. I was in business!

Next, I invested in some small classified ads in the backs of trade magazines for fitness professionals. Some worked and some didn't. I expanded the ones that worked. At this point, the business was bringing in enough for me to produce a hard-copy training manual, instead of just an e-book.

From there, I contacted some fitness associations and got approved to offer continuing education units to their members. At the same time, they agreed to let me write some articles about boxing fitness for their members. That helped the business to be more credible, and it grew substantially.

After the boxing program became successful, I repeated the same process by finding other fitness experts and rolling out certification programs with them. Some of them were very profitable and some weren't. However, I never spent more than $1,500 to develop any of them, so my risk was low. Each program has covered its initial investment and continues to be profitable five years later.

Andrew Mason, the founder of the coupon site Groupon, also used this approach of testing until success. He ended up building his business into one of the fastest-growing businesses of all time. Groupon had 400 subscribers in December of 2008, and grew to 44 million subscribers within two years, to the point that Google was willing to pay $6 billion for the company. I won't predict whether lower-cost rivals will eat into Groupon's market share, or whether Andrew and his investment team will one day kick themselves because they rejected Google's offer. Regardless, the company's incredible start-up trajectory still has plenty to teach us.

Before developing Groupon, Andrew ran a site called ThePoint.com. People used the site to organize protests, fundraising, or boycotts. If enough people committed, the campaign would happen. The site didn't work. He decided that he needed a simpler, more focused idea, with a clear revenue model. Groupon followed. It still uses the tipping point idea of gaining commitment from a critical mass of people, but now it focuses exclusively on coupons from local businesses.

There are many lessons that Groupon teaches, but one of them is that you never know what you will find out when you test your business. Groupon exists because its founder tried something that didn't work in one market but that did work in another. He kept working with the idea of a tipping point and applied it in a new form until his business took off like no other business ever had before.

The idea of a testing lab doesn't only apply to online businesses. For instance, if you are starting a professional services firm, testing might be the key to attracting your first customer and building momentum from there. My own consulting practice started out as a failure, until I got in front of as many people as I could to refine my target market, solutions, and marketing message. When I first started out, I couldn't get anyone to hire me. I figured I had all the right pedigrees and was smart enough to handle any problem that an entrepreneur or executive had. Unfortunately, nobody else agreed with me, and I didn't get anywhere after three months of trying.

I finally got the message while meeting with a potential client and referral source for coffee. She seemed frustrated during our whole meeting. Eventually she blurted, "Candidly, I have no idea what you do, what sets you apart, and what kind of person would be your client. I don't know what to tell someone about you, or even who to tell."

That was the most valuable business feedback I ever got in my life, even though it hit me like a sledgehammer. After that meeting, I decided to focus on three markets that I knew: non-profits, small technology start-ups, and healthcare companies. I crafted marketing messages for each one, focusing on the unique problems and requirements for each market. Then I reached out to people I knew in each market. Within a week I was invited to give a strategic planning seminar at a local non-profit support center. That seminar got me my first two clients in the non-profit market, and many more followed from there. I enjoyed similar success in the other markets I was targeting, too. Within six months, I was earning enough part-time as a consultant and coach that I was ready to quit my full-time job for good—along with my long commute and quirky boss.

Keep testing. Keep the things that work. Tweak or eliminate the things that don't.

Build the business in your spare time based on these tests, until you get that first profitable customer—or at least a promise from a customer that they will hire you when you formally launch your business. Try out free or very low-cost marketing tactics until you refine your marketing message and plan to become visible in the market. Sell prototypes and samples to prove that there is demand for your product before you go into production. Take one small step, then another, and then another. There will be steps forward and steps back, but if you keep working at it—without taking huge risks—you have an excellent chance that things will come together.

---

## AN ENTREPRENEURS' ADVICE ABOUT TESTING

*Test your idea with your target customer BEFORE you start spending money on your business—determine if what you will offer, at the price point you want/need to charge, is attractive to your target customer. If it is, rock on! If it isn't, find out why it isn't and make adjustments; then test again. Not until you KNOW people want to buy what you have to sell, and at the price you want/need to charge, do you have a viable idea.*

Stephanie Hackney, Chief Brander, Branding Masters
www.brandingmasters.com

# THE SIX BEST TYPES OF MARKETING
# TO GET YOUR FIRST PROFITABLE CUSTOMER

For decades, the *Guerrilla Marketing* series of books has provided readers with thousands of different ways to market their businesses. At the same time, the Internet has opened up—and continues to open up—entirely new ways to make your business visible to interested buyers. Thanks to both, you don't have to spend lots of money to get your new business off the ground and start reaching out to your market. Following are six broad types of marketing to consider before you invest lots of money in more expensive ways to promote your business.

**One: Referrals.** No form of marketing provides more bang for the buck than referrals. Even if you haven't had a single customer, your network of contacts can send a stream of business to your door. The secret to referrals is having the courage to ask the people in your network for referrals, and to have conversations that get results for you. Most people simply say something like, "I'm starting a new business. Please let people know." That approach is ineffective, because you are hoping that busy people will remember to talk about you, despite everything else they have going on in their lives.

A more effective approach is to ask your contacts to take some time to sit down with you and brainstorm about how you can help each other. Help them first. Ask them about the kinds of referrals and introductions that they seek and other ways you can help them in their business and career. Then, after you have helped them, educate them about the types of referrals and introductions that you want. Be as specific as possible. For instance, in my consulting business, I ask people to introduce me to executive directors of non-profits, especially those that might be struggling to set their strategic direction. You have to have a clear picture of who your ideal customer is, so that you can communicate it to others. Next, ask specific questions to help them think about people they know. For instance, if they are a member of Rotary, ask them who else in their Rotary group might be interested in your services. If you have a really strong relationship with them, you might even ask them to open up their contact database, and you can go through that together.

As you get names, ask how the other person would like you to connect. Will they make the introduction, or can you initiate contact? When you do get in touch, don't make a hard sell. Tell them that your colleague thought there might be a fit, but you aren't sure and wanted to see if it was worth a few minutes of each other's time to find out.

Finally, follow up to let the colleague who made the referral know how things went. You want these people to keep sending you referrals, and they take a risk whenever they do. Be sure to follow up either way, so that they continue to feel comfortable sharing their contacts with you.

Referrals don't have to be to potential clients. It can be equally powerful to get introduced to people who know lots of people, to people that might be able to provide resources and advice to you, and to people with whom you might form marketing alliances. For instance, if you are a business coach, you might form an alliance with a business broker so that both of you market to the businesses in your area.

Another key to referral success is volunteering and getting active in your marketplace. For instance, join industry associations. Serve on the board of prominent non-profits. Volunteer for popular community events, like the holiday parade or a big annual festival. The more active you are, the more people will see that you are credible and professional and will want to make introductions on your behalf.

**Two: Distribution arrangements.** If you can find a business that serves the kinds of customers you want to reach, you might be able to arrange a distribution deal that gets your products distributed widely in your marketplace. That's a fantastic form of leverage. For instance, I sell a book that helps physicians market their practices. I am always looking for distribution deals with medical supply companies. They can buy the book from me and give it to their customers as a premium. Similarly, if you are starting a fitness training or massage therapy business, try to get a contract with a large local employer or office complex to offer your services to their employees or businesses. You can provide a discount or special deal, while they promote you to their constituents.

**Three: Street marketing.** Street marketing consists of the low-cost, creative tactics that literally get you out on the street. They include posting signs on the sides of the road, offering free samples outside your store, passing your card out to other businesses, putting a sign on your door, handing out flyers, hosting an open house, and standing in the street with a big sandwich board. You can also put on some kind of publicity stunt that gets you attention in the media, for instance, by going for a world record related to your business or getting the community involved in some sort of fun event that you create.

**Four: Online marketing.** Online marketing opportunities continue to evolve and offer low-cost, potentially high-return opportunities for businesses. Your website, along with a blog, can form the center of your online presence. When you first start out, depending on your business, you may not even need to spend money creating a website, because you can get your business started via your social networking presence. You can create a free business page on Facebook and get your friends to like the page. You can build your LinkedIn network and get your colleagues to endorse you. You can tweet, start a free radio show on blogtalkradio.com, post videos on YouTube, post comments on other sites' blogs, get involved in online groups, post answers to questions on answer sites, contribute blogs to other sites, get freelance gigs on sites like Elance and oDesk, offer coupons on sites like Groupon, send out an e-newsletter to people in your contact list, and ask your colleagues to spread the word to their lists. If you want to spend more money, you can hire a social marketing specialist and a search engine optimization expert, and also invest in advertising networks like Google Adwords. The opportunities for online marketing continue to grow, and every entrepreneur needs to stay on top of them.

**Five: Educational marketing.** Educational marketing is especially useful to professionals who market their expertise, including consultants, coaches, attorneys, accountants, investment professionals, clinicians, fitness trainers, architects, engineers, piano teachers, and anyone else selling their knowledge and skills. Educational marketing tactics include speaking, giving tele-seminars and webinars, leading free seminars, writing articles and blogs, conducting and publicizing simple research studies, getting interviewed as an expert in the media, and sending press releases filled with short bits of useful information for your market. The concept behind educational marketing is that it takes time for people to perceive your value and see you as a credible expert. Nobody today wants a high-pressure sales pitch. However, they do respond to valuable information that helps them solve problems. Whether you promote educational events to your own list or get invited by the people in your network to speak or write to their constituents, educational marketing is a powerful way to get your name out there.

One tip: Anytime you provide educational content to other people, devise a way to capture their contact information so you can follow up. For instance, if you speak, give everyone in the audience a one-page sheet where they can provide feedback about your speech and also respond to a free offer you make to them. Offer them a free report, an assessment, or a subscription to your newsletter in exchange for their email address. That way, you can continue to stay in touch and invite them to other educational programs you offer.

**Six: Commission-only sales force.** When you are starting up, you might not have the time or talent to sell your products or services. However, you can hire one or two salespeople, or even interns, to sell your products or services for you. Many skilled salespeople seek part-time work, and some are willing to work for commission only, especially in a challenging economy. However, managing salespeople takes effort. You have to support your sales force with marketing collateral, prospect lists, and advice about how to close business. You might have to find one type of salesperson to get leads, while another closes deals, because those are different skills. Also, you might have to go through lots of people before you find one or two superstars who deliver results for you. By building a sales force while you get your business off the ground, even a small one, you create outstanding leverage on your time and start to grow a business that can run without you.

## CREATE YOUR START-UP MARKETING PLAN

To plan your strategy to get your first profitable customer, create your start-up plan. Use the template below. Choose at least five marketing tactics. Describe exactly what you will do, what your budget is, and a goal for the number of customers required for that tactic to be worthwhile. See the example that follows, and use it as a guide.

## YOUR START-UP MARKETING PLAN

| Tactic | The Plan | Test Budget | Goal |
|--------|----------|-------------|------|
|        |          |             |      |
|        |          |             |      |
|        |          |             |      |
|        |          |             |      |
|        |          |             |      |
|        |          |             |      |
|        |          |             |      |
|        |          |             |      |
|        |          |             |      |

| ILLUSTRATIVE START-UP MARKETING PLAN: | | | |
|---|---|---|---|
| **Tactic** | **The Plan** | **Test Budget** | **Goal** |
| Referrals | Speak to five people in my network every day. | $500/month to buy coffee or lunch. | 3 customers |
| Facebook | Have social marketing expert create a page for the business and ask friends to like it. | $50 for social marketing expert. | 1 customer |
| LinkedIn | Ask colleagues to endorse me; post updates on my profile. Reach out to contacts for referrals. Seek freelance work via LinkedIn. | $0 | 1 customer |
| Blogging | Create a website with a blog and email capability. Blog every other day. Tweet to my network and have it link to Facebook and LinkedIn. | $950 to set up the infrastructure. | 5 customers over the course of a year to pay for the initial infrastructure. |
| Elance, oDesk, Guru | Post my profile and start bidding for jobs. | $100/month to post bids. | 1 customer |
| Signs by side of road | Buy 200 signs and place them by the side of the road in my town to attract local business with creative approach. | $200 | 1 customer |
| Speaking at industry association | Get active in the association and give one speech per quarter. | $150 membership fee. | 1 customer |
| Writing articles in association newsletter | Write one article a month. | $0 | 1 customer |

# ADVICE FOR WHEN THAT FIRST CUSTOMER TAKES A WHILE

Sometimes it takes a while to get that first customer. That's why it is so important to take small steps and build the business as you go. You don't want to quit your job or exhaust all of your cash reserves until you are sure you have a business that works.

When that first customer doesn't come as quickly as you had hoped, there are five possibilities:

**One: Something about your solution is not quite right.** Ask other people for advice about whether your solution really solves the problems of the people in your target market. Ada Vaughan of CuteyBaby has built up a community of 1,500 moms who give her advice about baby products. She notes that many entrepreneurs only test out their products on themselves, which gives them a very limited data sample—and a biased one, at that. Get honest feedback from as many people as you can. Do your products and services offer a complete solution to the problem you are trying to solve? Do you provide everything your buyer expects in a total package? Do you offer the right support? The right price? The right terms? The right guarantee? Get objective advice, and adjust accordingly.

**Two: Your marketing message isn't influencing people to take action.** You might have a great product or service, but if your marketing message doesn't get people interested, you won't attract customers. Test different marketing messages. Emphasize the problem you solve and the primary benefits you provide. Give people both intellectual and emotional reasons to buy from you. Show why your offering is unique and better, and back up your claims with proof. Provide a guarantee or service pledge, so that buyers don't feel like they are taking a risk by spending their money with you. Remove every reason someone might have for not buying. Test different marketing messages and keep improving as you generate more interest.

**Three: You aren't working hard enough to get visible.** Remember, the best product is not always that one that wins. Hope is not a viable business strategy, and you can't sit back waiting for the phones to ring or your online orders to take off. You have to make marketing your top priority, especially when you are just getting started. Because he was a family acquaintance, I kept track of Paul Fireman when he was starting the shoe company Reebok. One thing that I clearly remember about him was that anytime he had extra money or time to spend on his business, he spent it on marketing. You should do the same—and if you don't have customers, all of your time should be focused on getting visible.

**Four: Everything is in place, and you have to stay the course and be patient.** Getting your first customer can feel like a long day of fishing. Sometimes you put the bait out and wait for hours. Just when you think you should call it a day or go to another spot, suddenly you catch a big fish. The first customer is the hardest and, if you have done everything right so far, he or she will show up eventually. When you first start up, it takes time and repetition for people to hear your message. If you have a website, it takes up to six months for Google and other search engines to recognize it and include it in their search rankings. Be patient, and keep going. Also, read the stories at the end of this chapter about how other entrepreneurs landed their first customers. Notice how many of them got their first customers through serendipity; two of them got their first customers simply by going to the post office! You never know when or from where that first customer will come. However, if you are active and keep moving forward, good things usually follow.

**Five: You need to go back to the drawing board.** There does come a point when you should stop what you are doing and go back to the drawing board. Only you can decide when that point comes. That's why it is important to set goals for your business early on, including milestones you need to achieve to continue investing your money and time in the business. The market is always right and, as the old saying goes, insanity is doing the same things over and over again while expecting a different result. If you don't get any people interested in what you are selling, and it is not because of the above-mentioned issues, you should consider the possibility that your business idea needs a makeover.

This doesn't mean that you give up the idea of starting a business and escaping your job. Remember that Groupon—and many other start-ups, including some of my own—emerged from the ashes of initial ideas that didn't work out. Meanwhile, we all know that Thomas Edison failed a thousand times before he invented a light bulb filament that worked. Take what you learned, keep what worked, and try again. If you have followed the advice in this book, then you have developed and tested your idea wisely, without betting everything on it or quitting your job impulsively. You still have time and your creativity on your side—along with much more knowledge about what works and doesn't than you had before. Keep trying, and don't look back!

---

# ENTREPRENEURS SHARE HOW THEY GOT THEIR FIRST CUSTOMER

**Tyler Sickmeyer, Director of Client Development, 5Stone Marketing:**

*When I launched my marketing firm, 5Stone Marketing, I was 22 years old, bold, and confident in 5Stone's ability to help small businesses. The first businesses I contacted were those with whom I already had a direct relationship, either as a friend, a patron, or both. Those relationships, coupled with the fact that 5Stone Marketing guarantees its work and promises to never raise rates on an existing client, landed our first few accounts, which are still with 5Stone Marketing to this day.*

**Scott Richards, CEO & Founder, Faceless Technologies:**

*The first client came when I began this company in 1998. I simply applied for a Director of Marketing Position with a smaller company that was grossing $5 million. I gave the interview performance of a lifetime, stressing that my number-one priority would be to reach every goal they had while also maintaining their budget. They called me in to offer me the position, and I told them, "My work begins with you today by saving you the money you would spend on my salary. Hire my firm to handle all of your marketing, utilizing the budget you already have, and that is all I need." I told them that at the end of the year, if I met or exceeded branding and financial goals they needed to reach, then they could pay me 50 percent of the salary they were offering to me. The rest is history.*

**Ellen F. Weiss:**

*As a new financial advisor seeking to build a CPA referral channel in a competitive market, I had to make a pitch that would make a great first impression! I baked gingerbread houses, totally from scratch, and packed them in house-shaped boxes with all of the candy and frosting to decorate them. I stickered up the boxes with our small company's logo and the message, "Let us help you get your clients' houses in order." Stringent rules for financial services make gifting really tricky in our business—most firms go with a mail-order gift basket with a card. Yawn! The response was enthusiastic and immediate—I'll continue this practice every holiday season.*

**Tangela Walker-Craft, Owner/President, Simply Necessary, Incorporated:**

*My first customers discovered my product, the GoPillow!, before it was even on the market. While exploring various shipping methods for my product, I went into my local post office. Two helpful postal clerks were attempting to help me find the perfect-sized*

*continued on next page...*

*...continued from previous page*

*box for shipping. While handling the GoPillow!, they asked, "What is this?" I told them about my product, and they both immediately said they wanted to buy one. I kept a copy of the check so that I would always remember where I got my first sale.*

### John Paul Engel, Knowledge Capital Consulting:

*I founded Knowledge Capital right after 9/11/2001 in a one-room apartment in New York City. I created a PowerPoint presentation full of useful information and sent it to everyone I knew. Within a few days I received an invitation to speak at a conference, where a managing director of one of the largest consulting firms in the world asked to meet me. They became my first client and have been a client ever since.*

### Mark Nelson, Chief Dog, ThumbDogs:

*We had no significant budget for marketing our new product, ThumbDogs, via the Internet, and so we went searching for free PR opportunities. We stumbled onto HARO, Help a Reporter Out, and started monitoring the listings over the summer. While I was on family vacation in Yellowstone in August, my wife and I scanned the daily email listings after the kids went to bed. My wife caught a posting looking for new gadgets for skiing. It was a perfect fit. I replied to the writer and bingo, he wanted to include our new product in his article for a national magazine targeted directly at our customers. Within one week of publication we received our first order, and the orders haven't stopped coming yet.*

### Crystal Brown-Tatum, President, Crystal Clear Communications:

*Landing my first marketing/PR customer required confidence, competence, and a strong desire to get the work! I was just laid off from a company, and one of my clients at the firm had always been impressed with my demeanor, professionalism and work quality. When they approached me about being a contractor I was floored, since I had never even thought about being a solo practitioner! I spent lots of time preparing for the initial meeting and did all of my research beforehand so that I could answer any questions and overcome any objections. Being prepared was the key and being competent was the welcome mat!*

### May Beltran, Artist, Illustrator, Graphic Designer, and Owner of Earth to Girl:

*I recently moved to a small town, La Grande, Oregon, and in March I started working for myself as a graphic designer, illustrator, and artist. Moving to a small town was a change for me, since I was accustomed to bigger cities in Southern California. In order to get to know different business owners in the small town, I personally visited each business that was of interest to me. One of them was a privately owned massage and skin studio. I booked an appointment and the business owner wanted to know exactly what I did. I told her about my business and showed her some of the cards I had illustrated. Immediately, she was interested in having me work for her to develop a new logo and some marketing collateral, as well as displaying some of my greeting cards in her shop for sale. Because I gave her business without expecting anything in*

*continued on next page...*

*...continued from previous page*

*return, she became my very first customer in La Grande and has referred me to many of her friends as well, leading to other design and illustration jobs. The power of good old word of mouth still holds true, especially in small towns and tight-knit communities.*

### Ani Papazyan BS, CN, LMT, Therapeutic Effect Plus:

*I was living in the United States for a couple of years, still learning English, fresh out of massage school. I met my first client at her hair salon. I saw her once a week for 13 years. When she agreed to pay $35 for an hour massage I was so excited, and I never raised her price. Every few years she would raise it by $5, and that was okay with me, even though my prices went up to $100-150 for an hour.*

### Andrew Hall, Founder, AMI Studios Inc.:

*I got my first customer nine years ago. I was looking through the phone book for businesses that might need a website. There were plenty of businesses who needed websites, but most did not want to spend the money to get one. I was cold-calling these people and getting rejected at every turn, but I was determined. Finally the manager of an art gallery said "I've been waiting for someone to call me," and I knew I was on the right track. This gave me the confidence to continue on, no matter how many rejections I experienced. I knew sooner or later there would be more people who were waiting for me to call them. After a while I got my timing and my pitch down, so that most of my calls led to a meeting with the decision makers and ultimately to a transaction. Cold-calling is one of the hardest forms of marketing to master, but anyone with a sincere desire to succeed can use it to their advantage.*

### Elene Cafasso, Enerpace, Inc.:

*It was almost nine years ago. I was still in coaching training. My last boss in Corporate America asked if I would coach her husband, who was a bit stuck in his career and trying to figure out what he really wanted to be when he grew up. It was a great blessing because it forced me to start coaching for income right away. Other coaches I trained with waited months or even years before they felt ready to jump in for money. I got a great client and my client figured out what would fulfill him as a career. Win-win!*

### Steve Silberberg, Owner, Fitpacking:

*Although I tried many different strategies and didn't know what I was doing, my first two customers responded to flyers I put up in local gyms. I run a business that guides people on backpacking adventure vacations to lose weight and get in shape, so I figured that targeting people who were interested in getting fit might be a good strategy. Ironically, five years and hundreds of clients later, I have never had another response from any other flyer I put up in a gym.*

### Janice M. Sellers, Owner and Genealogist, Ancestral Discoveries:

*I got my first customer with the first ad I placed. It was a free ad in the monthly newsletter of the local Mensa group I belong to. I felt like I had hit the jackpot. He stayed a steady customer for almost five years, until his health became very bad.*

*continued on next page...*

*...continued from previous page*

### Michael Sick, President, Sick Performance Concepts, LLC:

*I had just picked up my first packaged samples of the Surf-Grip and was standing in the line at the post office to ship samples out to a few distributors and resellers. I started talking to a lady in line, who ended up following me back to my car to buy a Surf-Grip for her son.*

### Diana Gardner Robinson, PhD, DGR Coaching:

*I got my first customer by accident! I asked a friend to let me dry run my introductory phone call with her because I was nervous about doing it live. We did the phone call. At the end I said, "I know this was supposed to be just a rehearsal but I really think..." and she interrupted me with, "Yes, I know. I want to hire you."*

### Tammy Gentry, Owner and CEO, CMD Gifts:

*I was shopping in a gift store and had my prototype of Penny Stones Ice Breakers in my purse. As I checked out, I asked the cashier if they were interested in ice breakers or conversation starters for their store. She said yes, and I pulled my prototype out of my purse and gave my first sales pitch. She loved the whole concept, packaging, and product. She let me know she was the owner of that store, as well as four more, and was connected with a distributor. I felt like I hit the jackpot! I'm thankful I didn't listen to my self-doubts as I decided to start the conversation; I would have missed my first big break.*

### Walt F.J. Goodridge, Founder, The Passion Profit Company:

*Inspired by the idea for a music industry how-to book, I wrote and completed the 250-page manuscript for Change the Game in four weeks. I created a spiral-bound copy at 3:00 am the morning of my flight to attend a music industry convention in Atlanta. During one of the convention forums, Getting Started in Music, I got up to the microphone, pitched and held up the draft copy of my not-yet-published book, and distributed flyers to those who were interested. By the time I got back home to New York three days later, there was already a check from one of the attendees in my post office box! My first mail order book customer! It felt fantastic! It was then I realized that my thoughts and words had real value! And I didn't even have an actual copy of the book, yet!*

### Marc S. Hyman, Colonial Heritage Solid Wood Floors:

*I got my first customer by placing ads in the For Sale section of Craigslist in major metropolitan areas. The ad had pictures that were linked to my website and offered our products at attractive prices. The ad resulted in hundreds of website visits and in several $2,500 plus sales.*

### Mark Chussil, Founder and CEO, Advanced Competitive Strategies, Inc.:

*At a conference about strategy I heard a gentleman ask the speaker a question, and I found the speaker's answer to be unsatisfactory. When the session ended, I*

*continued on next page...*

*...continued from previous page*

sought out the gentleman and gave him my answer. He liked it, and we talked about what I do—business war games and strategy simulations—and soon afterward his company became my first customer. Nice way into a Fortune 500 company.

### Mandi Dana-Panzer, CEO/Designer, Sweet Shoes:

I launched my business after ordering 500 pairs of infant shoes with a little of my own money. The shipment was on the water, so I had to sell them. I am a mother of three and had a job at the time, and so I had no time to sell. Every evening after the kids went down, I got on the computer and Googled baby stores. I set a goal to email at least 10 stores every night. Eventually, I picked up stores that are still some of my best customers.

### Kennison Kyle, Portrayer of Santa:

I was in a fabric store buying the fabric and fur needed to have a custom Santa Claus suit made. The lady ahead of me in the checkout line saw the fabric and fur then asked if I hired out as Santa. When I replied yes, she asked for my card. I didn't have business cards yet, so she wrote my name and phone number on the back of her receipt. She booked me for several years, as well as referring me to others, including the local Salvation Army.

### Ann Middleman, Principal, ADM Marketing & Research Consulting:

I went to a meeting of a professional association of business communicators, the IABC, and met an advertising executive who said he helped clients with branding. I introduced myself and said I conducted research for branding objectives. I followed up a couple of weeks later, as he requested, and left a message. He called me back and invited me to a business pitch with a client who wanted to conduct customer research. We won the business, and that got my company started.

### Barbara Schantz President & CEO Baby Dipper, LLC:

I had taken an eight-week FastTrac course at our local Women's Business Center of North Alabama, making some good local contacts and learning many new strategies for getting my business off the ground. During this time I was working with a web designer to get my website ready to present to the public and take orders from customers. Well, before I even knew that the site was ready to accept orders, a classmate from the FastTrac course placed an order through the site! I delivered his order in person to thank him for being my first customer. It was actually kind of scary to know that things were finally moving forward for my company, yet it was exciting and energizing at the same time.

## Chapter Ten

# BATTLE NUMBER TEN:

## Keep Going Until The Business
## Achieves Momentum

ongratulations! You have won nine of the ten battles required to quit your job and focus full-time on your business. Your final battle is to grow from your first customer to having enough customers that you feel confident enough to quit your job.

Follow these eight steps to win this battle:

**One: Improve the numbers.** At this point, you should have some useful data about how your business really works. How much time and money do you have to spend to get a customer? How many leads does it take? How much does the average customer spend when they buy something from you? How often does a customer buy? How much gross profit do you earn on every purchase?

Now you can set goals and test ideas to improve the numbers. For instance, my wife Elena's business, Moms on Edge, was doing very well when it first started. However, the average customer only spent $26 on the site. Elena wanted to see if she could increase how much customers spent when they came to the site, so she tested both free shipping and offering a free product if customers spent more than a certain amount. She also offered a Sanity Pack that, at $99, bundled her most popular products at a discount.

Next, she decided to launch some products that cost over $200. Elena started up a new site, www.etiquettemoms.com, that trains moms to offer etiquette classes. This site ended up being a huge success and raised her revenues and profit margins significantly, while also requiring much less effort to run than a website offering manufactured products. As a result of this success, she focused on offering other training programs to moms interested in teaching children's etiquette, teen etiquette, business etiquette, and arts and crafts.

She also continued to test new marketing strategies to find more profitable ways to generate leads, including social media, print advertising, and publicity—while also evaluating all of the data she gathered from Google Adwords to make her online pay-per-click advertising more profitable. Finally, she developed initiatives to entice customers who bought one program to buy others.

With these strategies, Elena has been able to triple her company's sales and profits in a few short years.

---

## AN ENTREPRENEUR'S ADVICE ABOUT TRACKING KEY METRICS

*Gather and review the key metrics for your business every month. If you are not measuring against past performance and your business plan, you are not in a position to make your business profitable. I was thrown out of my house at age 17 and started an auto repair business right out of high school. From that business, I created an auto salvage business that gradually grew from one employee to be one of the largest in the Southeastern United States. Ford Motor Company eventually purchased my operation. I have started, grown, and sold several businesses to Fortune 500 companies in my 30-year business career. I believe anyone can create a business if they plan, manage, measure the right metrics, and take action to improve those metrics.* —**Ron Sturgeon**

---

**Two: Build on marketing that works.** In the last chapter, you created a testing lab to try out marketing campaigns on a small scale. As your business gets traction, you learn which marketing campaigns are worth continuing, which are marginal and can be tweaked, and which are never going to work for you. In this phase of your business, you take successful marketing initiatives and roll them out as part of your overall marketing system. Expand them gradually, and continue to test and improve. You are creating a marketing machine that is guaranteed to generate profits for you on a repeatable basis.

**Three: Test new marketing.** You never stop testing marketing ideas. Make it a habit to test at least one or two new ideas every month. That way, you keep growing your business by finding new ways to attract and retain customers and increase your profits with each sale you make.

**Four: Keep getting advice.** Once you stop asking for advice, you become insulated, and your business will suffer. Therefore, don't stop involving your network, as well as your growing customer base, in your business. Get advice about ways to grow the business, new products and services to offer, new ways to differentiate your business from the competition, how to improve your customer service, how to attract talent, and any other pressing issues in your business. Involve your customers and email list in giving advice about new products and services you can offer, whether you contact a handful of people for a focus group, or send out a survey to your list via Survey Monkey or another free survey tool.

**Five: Get the operations under control.** There was a funny commercial that aired during the dot-com era in the early 2000s. In it, a group of entrepreneurs launch a website and sit by the computer screen, waiting for orders to come in. The business team cheers when the first few orders come in. Suddenly, a flood of orders comes in, and you see the team's facial expressions change. You know they are thinking, "How are we ever going to handle this volume?"

Almost anyone can handle a few customers by scrambling and improvising. As you get more customers, you need to develop infrastructure and put standard processes in place. Otherwise, you don't provide consistent service, customers complain, and your reputation suffers quickly—especially when customers can post complaints about you online to millions of people.

Therefore, list your most important business processes. Document each one, with specific quality and service standards. For instance, how quickly after an order comes in will you ship product? At what point will you order more inventory? How do you start up a new client engagement so that your client feels comfortable that you can deliver results? How do you handle common customer inquiries and requests? Your goal is to write everything down so that if something happens to you, somebody else can take over and run the business without you.

Once you have everything documented, improve. For instance, track the most common customer complaints and find ways to eliminate them. Set new performance goals to serve your customers even better. Look at areas where you have lots of rework or make errors, and fix them.

This exercise is not trivial. For instance, how often have you visited a restaurant and received great service and food, only to be disappointed on your next visit? Even at the wonderful Ritz-Carlton restaurant in our town, we still experience varying service levels, depending on our waiter and the day of the week. The fact that the Ritz can be inconsistent, despite their world-renowned training programs, shows how challenging it can be to set you business up to provide reliable service to each and every customer. However, this challenge is a fantastic opportunity for you. Once you get your quality and service down to a science, you gain a significant edge over many of your less-meticulous competitors, and also earn an increasing base of loyal customers.

**Six: Automate where possible.** Software and online services exist to automate just about every aspect of your business, including bookkeeping, project management, order processing, payroll, bill payments, communicating with your virtual team, updating your website, delivering digital products, answering customer questions, following up with visitors who are about to leave your website, and demonstrating your product at the click of a button. Many of these products are affordable—even free. As you grow, keep automating your company to save you time while seamlessly serving customers.

**Seven: Set the stage for growth.** When you first start your business, you wear every hat there is, from CEO to janitor. Once your business starts to get traction, it is time to pass the hat. Start thinking about ways you can delegate key responsibilities in the business to others. What does your ideal organization chart look like once your business reaches the next level? Which positions can you fill now, and which will you fill later? At what revenue level can you add contractors or employees to take over key responsibilities? What results do you expect from each person on your team, and how will you communicate these expectations and follow up? If you want to grow a business you can sell, it is never too early to create your organizational chart.

Keep thinking about how you can entrust others to run parts of your business for you, while you focus on setting direction and achieving growth.

**Eight: Set a goal to quit your job.** At some point, you are going to have to make the leap. Straddling the fence between your day job and your business eventually becomes counter-productive. Something will have to give. At what point will you feel comfortable making the leap? How much income will your business have to be making? Only you can answer that question. Some people wait until they have replaced their full salary. Others don't even need or want to replace their full salary; they prefer the life of the entrepreneur so much that they are willing to sacrifice a bit of income for the satisfaction and flexibility of working on their own terms.

However, know this: Once you do quit your job and work on your business full-time, you might find that your sales and profits grow even faster than they did while you were working part-time. That's because now you have nowhere to hide. You can't dabble anymore. You have no choice but to focus all of your time and energy on the business. That kind of commitment makes amazing things happen!

## CHECKLIST FOR ACHIEVING MOMENTUM

|  | No | So-So | Yes |
|---|---|---|---|
| You are improving the numbers. |  |  |  |
| You are building on marketing that works. |  |  |  |
| You continue to test new marketing tactics. |  |  |  |
| You keep getting advice. |  |  |  |
| You are getting your operations under control. |  |  |  |
| You are automating where possible. |  |  |  |
| You are setting the stage for growth. |  |  |  |
| You have set a goal to quit your job. |  |  |  |

If you have reached this point in the book, and in your business, you have one thing left to do: Declare victory! The next chapter describes how to do this gracefully.

## Chapter Eleven

# DECLARE VICTORY AND CREATE YOUR PERSONAL JOB ESCAPE ACTION PLAN

In the last chapter, you set a goal for when you will be ready to give notice and escape your job. As soon as you achieve that goal, take some time to celebrate. I'm not just talking about a pat on the back. Have a party! You have done something that most people dream of doing, yet few people have the guts to do. You have gotten a business off the ground!

Now that you are ready to leave your job, do it gracefully. The people with whom you work are future customers, investors, employees, contractors, and referral sources. Don't alienate them! Even if you are angry at them, have no respect for them, and never want to see them again, make an elegant exit. Chances are that you will see these people again. For instance, one mortgage broker I know quit his job at a major bank during the housing boom and started a very successful mortgage brokerage firm. Five years later, after the bubble burst, his company collapsed and he needed to get back into the workforce. Thankfully, he had maintained great relations with his former employer and had no problem going back to work for them, in a better position than he had before.

First, go back to the introduction of this book, and review the legal guidelines presented there. Don't do anything that violates your employment contract.

Second, be aware of the benefits that you are giving up. How much will your health insurance cost through COBRA? Do you have other health insurance lined up? What about life insurance, disability, and long-term care insurance? You might decide that, at least for now, it is better to shift from full-time to part-time status just to keep your benefits going for a while.

Third, if you have a retirement plan through the company, learn about what you have to do in order to roll it over to your personal account without any penalties.

Fourth, know your rights with respect to any vacation or sick days you have accrued. Use those up before you leave, especially if you can't convert them to cash.

Fifth, before you announce that you are leaving, anticipate what your boss will say and do. How is your relationship now? Will your boss try to negotiate with you? Or will he see you as a competitor and wish you anything but success? Will he be angry, calm, or overjoyed? It is important to be prepared for any objections, threats, or counter-offers. Also, decide ahead of time how much, if anything, you will disclose about your new business; in some cases it makes sense to tell your boss nothing other than that you are leaving to spend some time on your own and seek new career directions.

Sixth, be diplomatic. Thank your boss for the experience and all you have learned from him and from your job. Even if he is upset or angry at you, be positive. Give him enough time to make a smooth transition. If you end up staying for a couple of weeks after announcing your departure, don't become a distraction. Keep your head down and do your work until that blessed last day.

Finally, be equally graceful with everyone else in your company, along with vendors and customers. If you have been professional while working there, you might be surprised at how many of these people want to stay in touch, help you with your new venture, and even jump ship to join you.

I guarantee one thing: Once you announce that you have launched a business—whether on the day you resign or after you have left—more than a few people will either say or be thinking, "Gee, I envy you. Someday, I'm going to start a business, too." But unlike them, you know that there is no Someday. You get to live in the real world, where our dreams come true when we muster up some courage, take one small step, follow it with another, and keep moving forward from there. Again, congratulations!

# ENTREPRENEURS SHARE THE MOMENT WHEN
# THEY PULLED THE TRIGGER AND ESCAPED THEIR JOB

### Jack Liu, Chief Community Officer for TeenBusinessForum.com:

*I quit my job one month after I came back from a mission trip to Nepal. There, I saw real poverty and the only people that survived were entrepreneurs who had small enterprises. I realized that being able to start businesses, and failing until I succeed, is not only a privilege in the United States, but a responsibility. Knowing that I had the resources that I did, I had to go start a business that would create jobs and change the world.*

### ReeRee Rockette, Owner, Rockalily.com:

*I knew I was ready to make the leap when the dress code restrictions were tightened. It was the final straw, and suddenly I knew I was ready to leave my full-time job. I was tired of having to disguise my creative character, for instance, by hiding tattoos and not using bright hair dyes. The day after the new rules were distributed, I handed in my notice. I wanted to be able to celebrate who I am, rather than trying to hide it beneath a corporate uniform.*

### Jennyvi Dizon, Bridal and Evening Gown Designer:

*I quit my job as an Accounting Manager at a local magazine after the so-called CFO lectured me and made me cry for the last time. I was booking custom wedding gown orders left and right and felt that it was a sign for me to venture off into the fashion/wedding world full-time.*

### Nadine Peltier, Founder, Peltier PR:

*I worked at a major PR company, and I asked for a raise after bringing major accounts to the company and performing very well. I was denied the raise and something clicked at that moment. I was doing the work but getting paid very little. I thought that I could be doing the same amount of work and getting paid directly. I had all the ingredients of persistence, determination, courage, and focus. I quit within two weeks. The minute I put myself out there, I started getting clients. Within three weeks I more than tripled my income and am representing artists under Def Jam, Interscope, and other major accounts.*

### Jordan Harbinger, Managing Partner, The Art of Charm, Inc.:

*I quit when I realized: 1) I hated the field of law, especially real estate finance, and was only doing it for the money; 2) I saw YEARS of long hours working for clients whom I would NEVER meet, only to; 3) Perform a service for them that doesn't affect anyone personally in any positive way; and 4) The market turned WAY down and I saw my opening and took it. Severance was our startup capital. My former employer, a 160+ year-old law firm, closed its doors for good about a year later.*

*continued on next page…*

*...continued from previous page*

### Peter Laudin, The Pattycake Doll Co. and www.SleepySoft.com:

*I had spent 15 years employed with a company and had been building my Internet doll stores for eight. About three years ago I asked to go to a 32-hour week, so that I could devote more time to my own business, while maintaining a decent enough paycheck and in particular, the good health plan. Then last year four things happened at the same time: My business growth had hit a wall, because I just didn't have any more "free" time to work on it; my bosses threatened to make me go back to 40 hours because I wasn't making my quota; my daughter graduated college, which meant I couldn't keep her insurance coverage; and I got my annual Social Security letter estimating my benefits. I then realized that I would have to work for these a\*\*holes for as many as thirteen more years. No way! I gave notice.*

### Loretta McNary, TV Talk Show Host:

*The trigger for me was when people started coming to my desk at work, saying, "I saw you on TV last night!" My boss was not pleased with the attention or the extra traffic to my desk. He also stopped giving me special assignments once I told him about the show. Everything changed. Sometimes you just have to close your eyes and jump.*

### Jen Cadmus, Founder, The Dialog Lab:

*I was working 14 hour days and was a slave to my career. I love what I do, but if I am going to put in the time, why not have it be for my own business? I bought entrepreneur books and sought advice from every person I could get in front of, all advising me to have clients on board and a million ducks in a row before taking the leap. I always had the sound of my parents in one ear, worrying about me quitting my high-paying, stable, high-profile job. I finally realized, if you are a dedicated person, you can't get your ducks in a row and put all your passion into something when you are tied to supporting someone else's business. I stopped listening to everyone else and finally listened to my own gut. I took the plunge, never looked back and have never been happier. If you want it badly enough, are good at what you do, and have a legitimate business model, you'll make it happen.*

### Kristina Libby, Principle, KMV Media:

*At the point that my freelance work was making double my salaried job, I had an instant revelation: Quit! It was simple. I loved the freelance work and loved the increased profit.*

### Jeremy Shepherd, PearlParadise.com:

*My pearl business had reached the point where it was generating more income than I was making as a flight attendant. It was the best decision I could have made. Within a few months, my monthly income was greater than my yearly income with the airline. My company now does millions of dollars per year in sales.*

*continued on next page...*

*…continued from previous page*

### Dan Nainan, Comedian/Actor/Voiceover Artist/Computer Genius:

*I was a senior engineer with Intel Corporation. My job was to travel the world with Chairman Andy Grove, doing technical demonstrations on stage at events, and I was incredibly nervous about speaking on stage. I took a comedy class to get over the fear, and the comedy kind of took off. Since then, I have performed at the Democratic National Convention, at three presidential inaugural events, and I just performed for Donald Trump. Also, I appeared in an Apple commercial last year. I pulled the trigger when I got promoted to a really boring job. I was stuck in a home office, with no social interaction, no playing with technology, and no travel. I left after one year in that job.*

### Jack Eisenberg, CEO, MapDing:

*I recently left my job to pursue my tech startup full-time. I knew it was the right time when three things happened: I received enough funding to pay my expenses for six months; I went to a lecture by Mike Evans of Grubhub.com where he said that Step Zero of any successful business is to quit your job; and I got an ulcer from the stress of managing a full-time job and a full-time startup. It has been a great move, and the freedom to focus my energies has unleashed an incredible amount of opportunities, marketing and otherwise.*

### Thomas Farrell, Founder & VP of Client Relations, PEO Spectrum Inc.:

*For months I was losing my passion at my nine-to-five job. Immediately upon leaving the office every day, my mind would be fixed on my venture, and I'd work on it until I couldn't keep my eyes open. After enough planning I had to see if what I was dreaming up was even desirable in the marketplace. I made some beta sales calls, pitching our service without even having a mechanism to deliver the service. As it turned out, people were very interested and wanted to learn more. It was at this point that I knew without a doubt that we would have revenue the second we could deliver, so I left my job and started living the dream.*

### Shannan Hearne, Owner, SuccessPromotions.com:

*I had been running my company, Success Promotions, out of my home part-time for 14 years. I was working 60+ hours at a day job, never saw my kids, and was asked to take on one more volunteer position with our high school marching band program. I crunched some numbers, kissed my job goodbye, and never really looked back. But knowing that my oldest was leaving for college soon, I decided that if I was ever going to work from home full-time, I better get serious and do it.*

### Jesse Waites, www.BeaconHillApps.com:

*I quit my job to start my business when I realized my bosses didn't give a damn about me, and my bosses' bosses didn't give a damn about them. I make way more money now on my own.*

*continued on next page…*

*...continued from previous page*

### Carol Sankar, RRC d/b/a Carol Sankar Enterprises:

*MY INDEPENDENCE DAY!! I was working as a Paralegal in a mid-sized law firm in Uniondale, New York when I realized that I was worth so much more than my paycheck. I was being ordered around by a woman who had barely completed high school and who would insult me day after day. The feeling of biting my lips so I could get my paycheck on Fridays was beginning to take its toll on my happiness. I started working on my consulting business on the side, not realizing that I was an entrepreneur. The business started to pick up, and my bank account began to overflow, so after six months of biting my lips, on the weekend before Independence Day, I opened my mouth one last time and said, "I QUIT!"*

### Colleen Francis, Founder & President, Engage Selling Solutions:

*I decided to quit and get my business going when I realized I was harboring resentment for my Sales VP. He was a terrible leader and stereotypical old school sales guy, and I resented that for every dollar I made in commissions, he made $2. The last straw came during a joint sales call when he looked up from his presentation, put his hands on his hips, made little pistols with his fingers, and said to our prospect, "How do you like me so far?" Right then I knew that I could do better without him and it has become my mission to rid the world of salespeople like him though my sales training company, Engage. I quit within two months.*

### Shannon Lucier, Owner, Monster Graphics:

*The specific event for me was when I posted a small classified ad in a screen printing forum and saw that my services were in demand. I realized I could manage my own clients instead of working in an art department for minimum pay. I couldn't believe how many people were contacting me that first week from that one advertisement. It really blew my mind, and I worked double time for a few months saving money and defining my business before quitting. I even negotiated with the company I worked for and continued to do jobs for them on my own, as a 1099.*

### John Ivester, President, Advance Notice, Inc.:

*On the way home from picking up my updated resumes from a print shop I stopped at a car wash. While cleaning out the assorted trash from the car before vacuuming, I picked up the package of brand-new resumes, looked at them and decided that if I was going to start my own business, it was now or never. I pitched the resumes in the barrel and opened my own ad agency.*

### Deb Legge, PhD, CRC, LMHC, InfluentialTherapist.com:

*Eighteen years ago I was working half time for a New York State agency—a safe job with great benefits—while starting up my private counseling practice. I got to the point that I could not see one more client in the week without dropping all of the balls I had in the air at the time. I knew that I didn't have quite enough clients yet*

*continued on next page...*

*...continued from previous page*

*to make up what I'd lose by leaving the State. I also knew that if I didn't leave those golden handcuffs, I'd never really have the private practice I wanted for me and my son. It was time to go big or go home. I went big and never once looked back or regretted it for one minute.*

**Stephanie Seacord, Leading Edge:**

*I was the golden girl of corporate communications and director of PR for all 42 hotels at Omni Hotels North America, reporting to the President. Every review I got said exceeds expectations, 5 out of 5 points, blah blah blah. Then they made a new Senior VP of Marketing my boss. After months of trying to guess what he wanted, I asked him straight out. He told me, "I always wanted to be a football quarterback but recognized when I was in college that I just didn't have the talent for it. Some people are meant to be PR people. You are not." Then he gave me a 2 of 5 on my review, in spite of the fact that I made all my goals. I met with the President of the company and spread five years of reviews out in front of him. They said: "Great!" ..."Great!" ..."Great!" ..."Great!" ...and, in the fifth year, "Sucks!" I said to him, "When you can explain this to me, I'll be ready to listen." He couldn't. I wrote a letter of resignation that day and started doing PR consulting for individual hotels, travel, tourism and destinations a month later.*

# CONCLUSION:
## A Network of Entrepreneurs Wishes You Well and Reminds You that You Can Do This!

The purpose of this final chapter is to let you know that there is an entire world of entrepreneurs out there, and we are cheering for you. We are a not-so-underground army of Guerrillas. Because the media focuses mainly on covering the Fortune 500 companies, you might not realize that there are tens of millions of us. Some of us might even be your neighbors, building our businesses quietly—and happily—from our home offices, basements, or garages right next door to you. Whether you know it or not, we are here, working to fulfill our dreams, and living life on our terms. If we ever got organized into a serious political group, we could take this country over—especially since we create so much of the wealth and contribute so much of the tax revenue on which our political system depends.

We encourage you, we salute you, and we want you to succeed! We want you to leave a job that you don't like. We want you to be more successful and fulfilled working on your own business. We want you to live the life you want and deserve.

In fact, my personal goal in writing this book is that ONE MILLION people read it and take action to leave their jobs forever by starting successful businesses with little or no risk.

You can do this! I've reminded you again and again in this book, Jay reminded you in the preface, and you've heard it from the many entrepreneurs who have told parts of their stories and shared their wisdom in these pages.

Following is one last set of reminders, in the form of encouragement from others who have been in your shoes and taken the leap. Read their advice, and then take one small step towards making your escape. Do it today.

### Walt F.J. Goodridge, Founder, The Passion Profit Company:

*No employer will ever be able to pay you what you're really worth, because what you're really pursuing is not money, but the freedom to live life on your terms, and this is infinitely more valuable than any paycheck or pension. Reclaim your power, break free, and live true to yourself!*

### ReeRee Rockette, Owner, Rockalily.com:

*Imagine how you want to be in five years' time. Make the necessary changes now so that five years down the line you reap the benefits.*

### Jennifer Scully, ReDesign for a Dime:

*Let your passion guide you toward your dream job and never work again.*

### Robin Palmer, President, My Successables, Inc.:

*I worked as a Long Term Care Insurance Marketing Specialist and felt like I was donating my blood there every day, and not for a worthy cause. I was offered a position elsewhere, with an annual salary of $220,000 and I turned it down to start my own business! My advice: Envision yourself living out each option. You'll know!*

### Jesse Waites, www.BeaconHillApps.com:

*The working world will still be there for you if you ever decide to return. You can always go back to working for the man, so take a risk.*

### Sarah Yost, Breathe Life Coaching:

*If you've done the work and you're ready, quit refiguring things on paper and looking for all the ways you might fail. Just go.*

### Angil Tarach-Ritchey RN, GCM; Owner/Director, Visiting Angels.

*It's a huge leap of faith, but if you're passionate about it, LEAP!*

**Beverly Solomon, Creative Director, musee-solomon:**

*Have enough money to survive for at least two years and enough confidence, tenacity, faith, and vision to last a lifetime.*

**John Moore, PersuasionJujutsu.com:**

*Step out and do something great. Your comfort zone is a coffin.*

**G.V. Stelzenmuller:**

*Riding in the back of a drafty old van, cold and restless? Get up and drive—the scenery's better.*

**Nat Wasserstein, Lindenwood Associates, LLC:**

*One of the critical success factors in any new venture is understanding that the occasional poor decision will lead to good judgment in the future.*

**Michele Howe, Women's Health & Lifestyle Writer, Author of *Burdens Do a Body Good*:**

*Take the next appropriate step even if you feel afraid, and get comfortable with being uncomfortable as you move forward.*

**Mandy Williams, aka Black; Red & Black Books, L.L.C.; www.redandblackbooks.com:**

*Ask yourself if job security is an important consideration. If it is, then ask yourself if you have more control over your job—and more importantly, your life—if you are working for someone else or if you are the boss.*

**Heidi Dent, President, Hirease Inc.:**

*Life is liquid evaporating fast under the hot sun. It's better to branch out as a river into new territory, with some rapids and some droughts, where you can flow rather than sit miserably in your puddle.*

**Wes Schaeffer, The Sales Whisperer®:**

*Do what's best for you when it's best for you, because your employer will do what's best for them when it's best for them.*

### Bonnie Buol Ruszczyk, President, BBR Marketing:

*Most of the time, we DON'T do things because of fear, so don't give in to it. Give your business idea a shot, and if it doesn't work, you can always go look for a job. But if it does, imagine the possibilities!*

### Jimi Gibson, Owner and Creative Director, FindYourBanana.com:

*Committing to a three- to six-month plan to exit your job will allow time to understand your target market and what they want, confirm the profitability of your idea, discover your competitive advantage, and gain valuable momentum. Suffering through a job you hate will rob your soul and make you a miserable spouse, friend, and parent.*

### Cassandra Allen, Founder of Bullhorn Gypsy, C. Allen Design, and Sadie Books:

*Dreams are not mirages; they are road maps. So follow them.*

### Hank Wallace, Atlantic Quality Design, Inc.:

*Don't just produce a quality product, but be a quality person. Your most important products are reliability, trustworthiness, honesty, competence, tenacity, and breadth, and these will provide you with not only a sale, but repeat business for decades.*

### Peter Leeds, Principal and President, Gabardine LLC, www.gabardine.com:

*Following your dream is a great motivator, but it's no substitute for doing the legwork that's required to ensure success—or at least mitigate failure. Study the market, the audience, and the competition, and then put together a business plan that factors everything into consideration—not just your passion.*

### Anthony Adams, The Hangover Cure:

*I worked for IBM out of college, got laid off, and then started my own dietary supplement company selling a hangover prevention supplement. I have customers worldwide, with virtually no marketing budget. My advice: I'd rather try and fail at something I am passionate about and at least know I scratched my own itch and followed my gut than sit back and allow others to dictate my life path for me via job promotions, which means increased stress and workload for just a little more pay. You have absolutely nothing to lose.*

### Scott Milliron, President/Owner, Bug Brigade, Inc.:

*Jump into your venture without fear of failure, but work at it as if you are petrified of failure.*

### Dan Ptak, Simply Postcards:

*When I was debating making the jump from a big marketing research firm to launching an iPhone app, this is what a friend told me: The only security you need is knowing that you will learn more where you are going than you could anywhere else.*

### Gloria Berthold Larkin, President, www.targetgov.com and Marketing Outsource Associates, Inc:

*Learn to breathe deeply. You'll need to do it on your first day on your own, when you sign the first customer deal, hire the first employee, sign the first bank loan, make the first mistake, see the first bank statement with six figures, fire an employee, celebrate your first year, and realize you are living your dream.*

### Stephanie Schwartz, Owner, Roadrunner Traffic School:

*Plan, plan, plan. Then be prepared to throw all the planning out the window. Nothing will be as you thought it would be; it will all be better!*

### Ashok Kamal, Co-Founder, Bennu, LLC, www.bennuworld.com:

*Passion should be at the center of your new business. It's the driver that will get you through setbacks and make the victories more meaningful.*

### Victoria Staten, Resigned from Group Vice President at Kenneth Cole to start her own business:

*It's better to go for it and possibly regret it from time to time than to hesitate until it's too late and live with the regret that you didn't. One feeling comes and goes, while the other weighs down your soul like a tether holding you back indefinitely.*

### Misty Young, Chairman of the Board, Squeeze In, Inc.:

*There is little point in dreaming small. Now is the time to dream big and allow the Universe to help you fill in your passionate details with new vision and energy—it comes together when you believe it will! In my own case, I left a lucrative, secure partnership and VP position in a solid marketing firm to buy a tiny hippie restaurant in the mountains. We're opening our third location in 90 days!!*

### Dee Fegan, Pheasant Field Bed & Breakfast:

*Don't burn any bridges behind you! Those people can be a source for your customers!*

### Noelle Abarelli, The Smart Mompreneuer:

*When I made the decision to strike out on my own, there were plenty of naysayers. The best thing I did was surround myself with positive influences. I networked with successful entrepreneurs and created an incubator that my business could thrive in. Success breeds success!*

### Davis Viera, Mentalist & Speaker:

*Success is hard. No one has ever said success without first saying sucks.*

### Lunell Haught, Haught Strategies:

*I walked away from a perfectly good job I simply didn't have the heart for any more. I could have stepped off a cliff, but I stepped out to important, meaningful work. What made it possible was planning, having work and contracts set up prior to leaving the job as well as a just-in-case next egg. I've been a successful solopreneur for 15 years.*

### Rob Basso, President and Co-Owner, Long Island Advantage Payroll:

*Embrace your fear of going at it alone with the faith and knowledge that you are the marshal of your soul and that your path will be like none other taken.*

**Lisa L. Diggs, Founder, The Catalyst Company, LLC:**

*You can't effectively do it all yourself, so do what you are best at and truly passionate about, and hire experts to do the rest.*

**Karen McCleskey, Licensed Counselor, Dr. Karen McCleskey, Inc.:**

*Summon up your courage to ask for help when you need it. Just remember this: If you don't ask, you're the first one saying no.*

**Arden Clise, Clise Etiquette:**

*You don't need to have everything figured out to start your business. You'll learn as you go, and that's the best way to learn. Just do it!*

**Deborah P. Meeker, Business Broker, Murphy Business & Financial:**

*When you feel your engine revving up with excitement at the obvious business opportunities ahead, and your boss is more concerned with office supply management, you know you just have to go out there yourself and do it right!*

**Jeff Bogensberger, M.B.A.; Co-Founder and CEO, SOCO Games:**

*Entrepreneurs are like fisherman; they pretend to be secretive but they really just love to talk about their passion. If you are afraid to start because you don't know how to run a business, just ask and you will get detailed step-by-step instructions on everything you need.*

**LeAura Alderson, CEO, My Trainer Fitness:**

*Our trademarked slogan for our fitness clients applies equally well to entrepreneurs: Never easy...always worth it!™*

**Sharon Blaivas, www.ShakeUpMyResume.com:**

*Why are you here? Do you work to live or live to work? Take the opportunity to begin to live! Don't use life up working! Be your own boss!*

### Rashi Elmaliah, Director, Seital Group:

*Your reputation, not your product portfolio, is your greatest asset. Your best clients will likely come from other happy clients and from opportunities you discover along the way.*

### Ryan Merket, Founder and CEO of Appbistro:

*Embracing life is about doing what truly makes you happy. Being able to control your own destiny is both exhilarating and terrifying, but if it's in your blood, it's a yearning that can't be ignored.*

# ABOUT THE AUTHORS

**JAY CONRAD LEVINSON** is the author of the best-selling marketing series in history, "Guerrilla Marketing," plus 58 other business books. His books have sold more than 21 million copies worldwide. His Guerrilla concepts have influenced marketing so much that his books appear in 62 languages and are required reading in MBA programs worldwide.

He was born in Detroit, raised in Chicago, and graduated from the University of Colorado. His studies in Psychology led him to advertising agencies, including a Directorship at Leo Burnett in London, where he served as Creative Director. Returning to the USA, he joined J. Walter Thompson as Senior VP. Jay created and taught Guerrilla Marketing for ten years at the extension division of the University of California in Berkeley.

A winner of first prizes in all the media, he has been part of the creative teams that made household names of The Marlboro Man, The Pillsbury Doughboy, Allstate's good hands, United's friendly skies, the Sears Diehard battery, Morris the Cat, Mr. Clean, Tony the Tiger, and the Jolly Green Giant.

Today, Guerrilla Marketing is the most powerful brand in the history of marketing, listed among the 100 best business books ever written, with a popular website at www.gmarketing.com. It also powers The Guerrilla Marketing Association—a support system for small businesses.

Although Jay is able to list those notable accomplishments, he believes that the most notable is that since 1971, he has worked a three-day week from his home.

After living in the San Francisco Bay Area for 35 years, Jay and Jeannie Levinson sold their home, bought an RV, towed a Jeep, and ended up six years later at their lakefront home outside Orlando, Florida and close to their

26 grandchildren—their own personal Disney World. Nobody on earth is as qualified to tell you about Guerrilla Marketing than the Father of Guerrilla Marketing, Jay Conrad Levinson.

**ANDREW NEITLICH** is the founder and director of Solo Revolution (www.solorevolution.com), a unique association of solopreneurs from around the world who are building businesses and living life on their terms. He is also the founder and director of the Center for Executive Coaching (www.centerforexecutivecoaching.com), along with sister organizations The Center for Career Coaching (www.centerforcareercoaching.com) and The Institute for Business Growth (www.instituteforbusinessgrowth.com). These organizations train coaches and aspiring coaches from around the world to work with executives and business owners. Andrew received his undergraduate degree from Harvard College in 1987 and his MBA from Harvard Business School in 1991. He lives with his wife Elena and three children (Noah, Seth, and Willow) in Sarasota, Florida, where he plays tennis almost every day.

Introducing … .

# THE JOB ESCAPE CHALLENGE

**WANTED: ONE MILLION PEOPLE WHO ARE SICK AND TIRED OF HAVING A JOB AND ARE READY TO START THEIR OWN BUSINESSES.**

**IF THIS DESCRIBES YOU, I WILL HELP YOU IN ANY WAY I CAN, STARTING WITH A PACKAGE OF RESOURCES VALUED AT $497.**

To take the Job Escape Challenge, go to www.JobEscapePlan.com right now and enter the password ESCAPE. That's all you have to do. There is no purchase needed. You will be invited immediately to a series of powerful teleconferences that will motivate you to do exactly what you need to do NOW to escape your job and start your own business.

PLUS, while you are on the site, take advantage of other resources there to help you escape your job, including Q&A directly with the author.

**Take the Job Escape Challenge. Go to**

# JobEscapePlan.com

**and log in now. The password is ESCAPE.**

REMEMBER—If you got value from this book, tell a friend or colleague about it. People will appreciate you for letting them know about a resource that can help them.

To learn more about Guerrilla Marketing
and Jay Conrad Levinson, visit

# www.gmarketing.com.

# BUY A SHARE OF THE FUTURE IN YOUR COMMUNITY

These certificates make great holiday, graduation and birthday gifts that can be personalized with the recipient's name. The cost of one S.H.A.R.E. or one square foot is $54.17. The personalized certificate is suitable for framing and will state the number of shares purchased and the amount of each share, as well as the recipient's name. The home that you participate in "building" will last for many years and will continue to grow in value.

### Here is a sample SHARE certificate:

## YES, I WOULD LIKE TO HELP!

*I support the work that Habitat for Humanity does and I want to be part of the excitement! As a donor, I will receive periodic updates on your construction activities but, more importantly, I know my gift will help a family in our community realize the dream of homeownership.* **I would like to SHARE in your efforts against substandard housing in my community!** *(Please print below)*

PLEASE SEND ME _____ SHARES at $54.17 EACH = $ $_____

*In Honor Of:* _____

*Occasion: (Circle One)   HOLIDAY    BIRTHDAY    ANNIVERSARY*

*OTHER:* _____

*Address of Recipient:* _____

*Gift From:* _____ *Donor Address:* _____

*Donor Email:* _____

**I AM ENCLOSING A CHECK FOR $ $_____ PAYABLE TO HABITAT FOR HUMANITY OR PLEASE CHARGE MY VISA OR MASTERCARD** *(CIRCLE ONE)*

Card Number _____ Expiration Date: _____

Name as it appears on Credit Card _____ Charge Amount $ _____

Signature _____

Billing Address _____

Telephone # Day _____ Eve _____

**PLEASE NOTE:** Your contribution is tax-deductible to the fullest extent allowed by law.
**Habitat for Humanity • P.O. Box 1443 • Newport News, VA 23601 • 757-596-5553**
**www.HelpHabitatforHumanity.org**